The HELIX Factor

The Key to Streamlining Your
Business Processes

By

Michael R. Wood

The HELIX Factor : the key to streamlining your business processes by Michael R. Wood

ISBN: 0-9659809-3-6

Library of Congress Card Catalog Number: 97-095060

First published in the United States in 1998 by The Natural Intelligence Press, P.O. Box 0785, Marmora, NJ 08223

Edited by Dick Cole, and Jerel Crosland.

Jacket design by ONE ON ONE Productions

For more information about Michael R. Wood, this book or other publications write to **The Natural Intelligence Press, P.O. Box 785, Marmora, NJ 08223**, or send email to Mike_Wood@MSN.COM

TO MY FAMILY

BEYOND ALL ELSE, THIS WORK IS A PART OF MY LEGACY.

IT IS NOT ABOUT MY LIFE'S STORY. IT IS ABOUT MY LIFE'S WORK.

AS YOU READ THIS BOOK, LOOK BEYOND THE DIAGRAMS AND THE TECHNIQUES. LOOK INSTEAD TO THE PHILOSOPHIES AND VALUES THAT I HAVE TRIED TO IMPART.

THINK ABOUT THE GIVING TO, SHARING WITH AND HELPING OF OTHERS THAT HAPPENS THROUGH, WHAT I CALL, **HELIX**

THANK YOU JANE, TARA AND HEATHER FOR ALLOWING ME TO BE A PART OF YOUR LIVES. I LOVE YOU ALL

Your Masterpiece

LIFE IS YOUR CANVAS,

YOU ARE THE ARTIST.

EACH STROKE OF THE BRUSH,

EACH COLOR CHOSEN, ADDS TO THE OVER ALL RESULT

LET

   YOUR CANVAS BE BROAD AND FULL OF POSSIBILITIES.

   YOUR PALLET ROBUST WITH COLORS OF LOVE, TRUST, CARING AND CHARITY.

   YOUR TECHNIQUE SUPERB WITH AN EYE TOWARDS THE FINISHED WORK.

REACH DEEP FROM WITHIN AND BEYOND YOURSELF.

GIVE WAY TO INSPIRATION.

PRODUCE A WORK THAT LIVES BEYOND TOMORROW.

PAINT WITH PASSION, PERSISTENCE AND PRIDE.

FILL YOUR CANVAS WITH BEAUTY, FAITH AND HOPE.

LIFE IS YOUR CANVAS,

YOU ARE THE ARTIST,

PAINT A **MASTERPIECE!**

TABLE OF CONTENTS

TABLE OF FIGURES

Preface   Why Call it HELIX

This book was written to provide people and organizations with the insights, principles and tools needed to align business processes with the visions and strategies they are pursuing.

When choosing a name for this approach, it was important to select something that serves as a metaphor for the method as a whole. The double helix is the spiral that comprises DNA in the body. In a sense it is a binding agent that makes life possible. The word helix also means to turn around. Both seemed appropriate for this method.

In a sense, HELIX is a binding agent that helps organizations maintain a balanced focus of stakeholder expectations. Its principle based approach serves as a foundation for making clear and decisive decisions from strategy through to work processes.

HELIX is also used to help organizations turn ailing practices around. Using the method, companies can quickly assess where misalignments exist and take corrective actions that are positive and constructive.

So like the helix spiral that holds the building blocks of life together, HELIX holds together the alignment building blocks an organization needs to support continuous growth and improvement.

ACKNOWLEDGMENTS

Many friends, colleagues and loved ones supported the effort to create this book. There is no way I could have written this book alone. So, I offer my thanks and appreciation to everyone who supported me especially those below.

To my wife Jane who tolerated my 5 am. writing sessions and patiently listen to me talk on and on about my aspirations for this work. You encouraged me to stay with the process even when it appeared to be more folly than quest.

THANK YOU MY LOVE

To Dick Cole, a mentor, who brainstormed with me throughout the process. You provided feedback and encouragement on each chapter as the book progressed. You organized a workshop to pilot the concepts and ideas in this book. You are a valued and respected friend.

THANK YOU MY GOOD AND TRUSTED FRIEND

To Jerel Crosland, an old friend, who took an interest in the book and exhibited true enthusiasm for its completion; You provided much needed insight, feedback and support.

THANK YOU JEREL

To Eileen Feretic, a very special thank you. Your comments, and professional insights helped me to produce a work of which I am truly proud.

THANK YOU, THANK YOU EILEEN

ABOUT THE AUTHOR

Pioneers are a breed apart from the average person. Their sense of vision and purpose drives them to explore; to find new ways of doing and achieving. By their nature they observe, question, reflect and create.

Michael R. Wood is a pioneer in the true sense of the word. His life has been a continuous quest toward finding new paths to improve, new ways to understand. "The HELIX Factor" represents just one facet of Wood's quest. It is the culmination of over 16 years of questioning conventional wisdom and accepted practices. It is based on years of reflecting on ways to improve how organizations do business. The result is an organizational alignment and business process improvement technique called HELIX.

Michael was born in San Diego in 1950. In 1966 he was introduced to Mastery concepts through the study of the Martial Arts. Michael graduated from the University of Southern California with a Bachelor of Science degree in Business in 1972. In 1974, he became a CPA. Immediately upon entering the professional ranks, Wood became immersed in accounting, consulting and data processing. In 1978, Michael began seeking ways to align the expectations and needs of an organization to the emerging information technology age. By 1981, he had developed a formal Systems Development Life Cycle methodology called "THE HELIX

METHODOLOGY". What differentiated this technique from others of the day was its focus on discovering organizational needs prior to defining solutions. At the time, the ideas were so radical that Wood received little recognition from the systems methodology community. However, his business clients embraced and benefited from his approach. His associates nicknamed him the TRUTH SEEKER.

During the 1980's, Michael continuously improved the methodology. His focus moved away from technology and toward aligning organization's strategic direction with their work processes.

As an educator, he served as an Adjunct Professor in Pepperdine University's MBA program and an Associate Professor at California Lutheran University. He has conducted workshops and seminars on a national and international basis for organizations like Penton Learning Systems and the California Society of CPA's.

As an involved professional, Michael has served on the Board of Directors of the Texas Instruments International User Group and the Financial Management Systems International User Group. He has served on the California Society of CPA's educational advisory board as well as the Editorial Advisory Board of Beyond Computing Magazine. He has been published in ComputerWorld, CIO magazine, Los Angeles Business Journal and other trade magazines and newspapers. He is often quoted as an expert source in periodicals.

Michael is a CPA. He has worked at the national firm level and as a partner at the local and regional firm level.

As an entrepreneur and executive, he headed up the successful Helix Corporation for over 6 years. During that period, Wood's clients included Golden Nugget, Hughes Aircraft, Warner Bros., and Western Communications. Michael's most recent assignment is serving as a key executive in a $300 million plus hospitality and entertainment corporation.

CHAPTER 1   THE QUEST

HELPING PEOPLE AND ORGANIZATIONS EFFECT POSITIVE OUTCOMES

The process of improving an organization's ability to do business and continually add value to its constituents poses a formidable challenge. Over the past 18 years, my QUEST has been to develop a set of techniques and approaches to meet this challenge. What I have learned is this: People posses the key. People use the systems. People perform the processes. Therefore, *People add the value* .

> **Effecting positive outcomes requires changing the way people think and do work. It means achieving alignment in form and substance, in principle and in action throughout the organization.**

Since resistance to change is a given, the key to improving processes is to develop a method that:

1. Taps people's creativity and knowledge,

2. Identifies where, how and why the improvements can be realized,

3. Builds consensus among those impacted,

4. Obtains emotional buy-in at all levels,

5. Generates momentum to achieve improvements,

6. Quantifies the criteria to measure the success of those improvements and

7. Specifies the actions needed to move forward.

This book presents the method known as HELIX. Development of HELIX began in the late 1970's. HELIX is a principle based approach that provides a foundation for making clear and decisive decisions that are consistent from strategic planning through business processes. It is logically sound while being consistent with human nature and the emotional needs of those affected.

HELIX is a complete work yet is continuously evolving and improving. The method has been developed under "real life" conditions, in the field on countless projects.

HELIX is a nuts-and-bolts approach that is deceptively simple in its presentation yet elegant in its conciseness and completeness. The method integrates systems theory, psychology, change and organizational analysis concepts into a facilitation, modeling and diagnostic process. Along with achieving the seven criteria listed above, HELIX:

1. Improves empathy and teamwork between cross-functional work groups,

2. Develops a framework for renewal and future business process improvement,

3. Enhances organizational learning opportunities by improving communications and dialogue among people, departments and divisions,

4. Generates the information needed to define and design related information systems in context to the business processes they support.

If there is one thing I know it is this: HELIX WORKS!

Outcomes from HELIX projects have far exceeded expectations. ***Typical returns on investment (ROI) range from 500% to 1,000%.*** At times, it is hard to believe that a technique that appears so simple can be so powerful. However, the number of projects that have been done and the results that have been achieved speak for themselves. From time to time, projects that have led to the perfecting of HELIX will be shared to help reinforce the results that can be achieved. Here are two examples:

Entertainment Industry

This major film company had spent two years attempting to create the requirements for a comprehensive new film marketing function. After two years and thousands of wasted hours, the company determined that the effort had failed. In addition, relationships between departments crumbled. Top management subsequently had terminated the majority of the project's team leaving junior level staff to carry on.

Helix Corporation was given the challenge to assist the company in saving the project. The revival began by first training the new team on HELIX, then coaching the team, on a real time basis, through the HELIX processes.

The result was the completion of the requirements document in three months and phase 1 of the implementation in sixteen months. How much did the new marketing environment save? That data was not available to the team. However, the savings over the prior failed approach were substantial (2 years and around 60,000 hours vs. 3 months and around 6,000 hours). The outcome was that HELIX was successful in 1/8 the time at 1/10 the cost.

Healthcare Industry

This medium sized mental hospital was on the verge of financial ruin. Regulatory reporting requirements along with inefficiencies in its operations had become overwhelming. Helix Corporation was engaged to assist the organization to redefine and redesign the majority of its business practices. The project team, coached by HELIX consultants discovered and implemented an environment that provided:

1. Redundancy free patient tracking and records management,

2. On-line collaborative treatment notes and

3. Reduced regulatory reporting costs from $ 5 million a year to about $100 thousand a year.

Over a 5 year period the regulatory savings alone exceeded $24 million or a return of about 49 to 1. Keep in mind that this happened in the early 1980's. In 1996 when the now retired CEO was asked to comment on the impact HELIX had on the hospital, he basically said, it saved the company.

All of this could sound too good to be true. If this is the case, try to suspend your disbelief long enough to absorb the essence of what HELIX is. HELIX is as much a philosophy as a methodology. Like learning a martial art, you will start by understanding how to emulate the techniques and work with the various forms. As mastery grows in HELIX, the practitioner will begin to internalize it as a form of thinking that transcends models and diagnostic techniques. The ability to think at a macro and micro level simultaneously will improve. Lateral thinking and active listening skills will also improve.

> **Many people will improve their ability to rapidly develop solutions to problems through the synthesis of variables instead of through traditional analysis techniques.**

Finally, the mind can be conditioned to sharply focus on essential issues quicker than ever before.

With all its potential, HELIX can also be a double edged sword. As you master HELIX as a thinking discipline, you might tend to find it difficult to be patient with others. What will appear as a self-evident truth, will often be as clear as mud to those around you.

> **Remember, that effecting positive change requires consensus and emotional buy-in be reached by those affected.**

HELIX is, at its heart, a process for helping organizations and people discover and achieve desired outcomes in business processes. Be careful to balance your improved lateral thinking and synthesis skills with the your improved facilitation skills.

A NOBLE JOURNEY STARTS WITH A COMPELLING VISION OF THE FUTURE

Chapter 2 Preparing for the Journey

Developing Context and Historical Perspective

Before journeying into the world of HELIX, a short trip through its history needs to be taken. This is important. A historical perspective will build a better understanding of HELIX.

For the most part, I developed HELIX. I say "for the most part" because HELIX has been influenced by many people and ideas over the years. Its evolution is as much a part of my personal growth as my growth is part of HELIX.

After working as a CPA (Certified Public Accountant) in a large national CPA firm for about 5 years, I became painfully aware that I did not enjoy accounting, tax or auditing. What I did enjoy was business consulting. While at the firm, I was given the assignment of managing two groups. The first group was the Small Business Services Department. Here I was able to work with a variety of businesses as a financial advisor and management consultant. This provided me with a complete view of how businesses are planned, managed and operated. Because of their modest size, it was possible to grasp the impact of the political, social and financial dynamics at work.

The second group was the Governmental Services Department. This was a financial consulting and data processing service bureau that provided services to local governments throughout Southern California. Here I learned about information management and the positive impact technology can have on an organization's productivity.

My first big consulting assignment came around 1976. The San Fernando Valley Board of Realtors (then the largest in the country) wanted to move from their IBM System 3 to an on-line database system. Their goal was to allow Realtors to dial into the database and search for homes that match the needs of prospective buyers. This was bleeding-edge stuff in 1976. Our solution, an HP3000 based system, was found in only a month or so and later implemented. First effort, first success. I immediately knew consulting was the career for me.

Wanting to pursue a career in consulting, I left the firm and found a local accounting firm that agreed to let me build a consulting practice. In exchange I would manage their small business clients and implement an internal client accounting and billing system. Within one month of starting, I met Dick Cole who was speaking to a group of CPA's. Dick Cole is a former IBM trainer who turned independent consultant, speaker and mentor to me. His main focus was to help executives understand the implications associated with introducing computers into an operational environment. His message focused on the human and technology issues of automation. In retrospect, Dick touched thousands of lives by helping organizations avoid the pitfalls associated with the poor implementation of information technology into a business.

Dick Cole became a major influence in my professional life. It was through Dick that a mutual synergy developed. His background in marketing and executive computer education, coupled with my budding ability to identify and implement business solutions, turned to magic. During that year, Dick met Ken Orr. Ken's claim to fame was his development of the Systems Design Methodology known as Warnier-Orr and today known as DSSD.

After attending one of Ken's workshops, I was hooked. Ken's method was based on two major elements. The first was a bracket diagramming technique developed by Dominique Warnier from Honeywell-Bull in France. Dominique, a mathematician, had published a book on systems design based on set theory and the use of 4 basic logic constructs. Ken had the book translated into English thus forming the Warnier-Orr bracket diagramming system. The second major element of Ken's methodology was his breakthrough idea that a system could be designed from its outputs backward. This logical approach to design was extremely simple and straight forward.

Adding this to my bag of tricks allowed me to tackle very complex projects. Now I believed I could aggressively analyze, design and implement solutions for business. However, I was turning into a systems consultant more than a management consultant.

In 1979, Dick introduced me to Bill Bearly. Bill was a professor at a local university. He held a masters degree in computer science and a doctorate in organizational behavior. Bill provided a major piece to a puzzle I did not know I was trying to solve. Bill provided the insights needed to begin understanding organizations as dynamic, living entities. The knowledge I received from Dick, Ken and Bill gave me the experience and desire to develop my own approach to helping organization's achieve major improvements.

In 1981, HELIX was officially born. Even though my consulting used some of the models, I had not really bundled the approach into a true method. It was in a retreat in Santa Barbara with some respected colleagues that the decision to develop HELIX was made. The name HELIX came from a brainstorming session where the group threw out names they believed reflected what the method was all about. After two hours it came down to HELIX.

Back then HELIX consisted of a series of models that were used interactively with an organizations knowledge workers (the people who do the work). The process developed a shared understanding of how business processes functioned and how they could be improved. Through the development of these models, a group of knowledge workers were able to identify where process improvement opportunities existed, what those improvements looked like (in context to how work was done) and how those improvements could be implemented. In that same year, I published an "In-depth" article in ComputerWorld describing this new approach. In essence, I had managed to combine all the different perspectives and techniques learned from Dick, Ken and Bill into a process improvement method.

The next big breakthrough came while teaching a system design course with Ken Orr to the State of California in Sacramento. Here, the concept that an organization can be viewed as a series of *Value-added Delivery Systems (VADS)* was born.

> **A VADS is a cross functional business process that must exist in order for an organization to successfully operate.**
>
> **Each VADS has a predetermined intent to deliver a specific outcome to one or more of an organization's stakeholders.**

This new paradigm was profound to me. It allowed me to approach business process improvement from an organizational and strategic perspective.

As success grew, I became painfully aware that I was a person in his early 30's advising companies, worth millions of dollars, to pursue major changes in their business practices and processes. What if my advice was wrong? Another page in the development of HELIX was turned. By incorporating a series of proof of correctness steps, HELIX became self-proving. As the then U.S. CIO of a major Japanese car manufacturer in Southern California put it, "Your technique has built-in acid tests." These "proofs of correctness" tests were completed during a series of diagnostics that correlated data from different models ensuring they were consistent and complete. The tests were designed to ensure that the recommendations were on target and right for the clients.

In 1983 with HELIX under my arm and a strong entrepreneurial spirit in my heart I formed Helix Corporation. At that same time I took on a business partner. Her name was Jody Martin, another Dick Cole contact. Jody helped me to package HELIX and improve it more.

For the next eight years my life was consumed with refining and perfecting HELIX. The company became one of the first consulting firms in Southern California to do fixed-priced process improvement and re-engineering projects. As one venture capitalist told us, "You are either way ahead of your time or insane." I thought a little of both was most likely the case.

Why am I writing this book in 1997? The quality movement has been recognized as a worthwhile pursuit. Yet, Total Quality Management is having problems and Reengineering has been directly linked to downsizing and downsizing has become another word for "You're Fired!".

People and organizations want an approach that delivers the goods. There has yet to be published an approach that is as quick and complete as HELIX. At the urging of many of my colleagues, I have decided to share HELIX. In doing so, I hope to share its potential to help organizations develop Value-added Delivery Systems that improve performance, efficiency and morale.

CHAPTER 3   THE ROAD AHEAD

PREVIEWING THE REMAINING TERRAIN

This book presents a road map for developing a working knowledge of HELIX. Like any worthwhile pursuit, mastery requires study and practice. With study and practice a person can become quite accomplished at constructing and diagnosing HELIX models. I recommend that if you have not done a great deal of group facilitation, you find a workshop where such skills can be experientially learned.

> **Facilitation and listening skills are critical ingredients to the HELIX recipe.**

This book and associated implementer's guide offer an approach to improving business processes. Chapter 4 **"Laying the Foundation for the Road Ahead"** focuses on 8 factors that represent the key principles upon which HELIX is based. Chapter 5 **"The Alignment Factors - Ensuring Interim Destination Points Connect"** presents 9 factors that must be considered when aligning an organization in form and in substance. Chapter 5 begins with key factors for aligning strategic direction to the needs of stakeholders. It ends with the importance of aligning value-added concepts to the transformation of information be shared. Chapter 6 **"Executive Overview - Managing the Process"** presents a high level view of the tools and techniques of HELIX.

It provides 4 major steps of a project from the executive briefing through presenting the project's findings back to management. This chapter is designed to help upper management understand the tools and techniques of HELIX at an appropriate level.

Each chapter provides guidelines and pragmatic examples to assist understanding and learning. At the end of chapters 4, 5 and 6 there is a short chapter summary and a series of questions for reflection. The summaries and questions are provided to reinforce the understanding of the material and to provide a quick reference for the future.

The principles and rules presented in each chapter will help resolve ambiguities that might be encountered during a project. The examples presented will serve as a quick reference to refer to during projects. Each example has been taken from real projects where HELIX was successfully deployed.

"The HELIX Factor II" is the companion book to "The HELIX Factor." It is an implementer's guide and case study intended for those within the organization who will perform actual projects. Through the case study virtually every aspect of HELIX will be presented. "The HELIX Factor II" provides everything a team needs to organize a project, deploy the appropriate tools and techniques, and conduct the facilitation and diagnostic work sessions.

When you have completed this book and the related implementer's guide, reflected and practiced a while, you should know how to:

1. Organize,

2. Analyze,

3. Correlate,

4. Document,

5. Manage and

6. Produce a completed HELIX project.

Your initial efforts should yield impressive results.

Try not to deviate from this map. Be pragmatic in your approach until you have mastered the models and their interrelationships. The temptation will be great to take short cuts. Resist the urge. Even when you follow every step, HELIX is very fast. If you approach HELIX as a purist, you will generate your best results.

> **Like a chef, you should not vary the recipe until you have a full command over the cause and effect that each ingredient has on the finished product.**

Let's go!

KNOWLEDGE WORKERS ARE
CONSCIOUSLY AWARE OF THEIR IMPACT
ON THE PROCESS.

CHAPTER 4   LAYING THE FOUNDATION FOR THE ROAD AHEAD

8 KEY FACTORS
THE PRINCIPLES THAT DRIVE HELIX

HELIX integrates a number of key factors that take the form of principles and organizational alignment concepts. These principles and concepts form HELIX's philosophical foundation. Through a complete understanding of these factors comes the judgment needed to deal with the dynamics present in any organizational or business process improvement effort.

When you live it,

you believe it!

FACTOR # 1

THE PRINCIPLE OF MAKING A DIFFERENCE

WE ALL MAKE A DIFFERENCE
THE KIND OF DIFFERENCE WE MAKE IS UP TO US

How many times have you heard people say, "You can't make a difference, so why try?" Listen, **We All Make a Difference.** The only question lies in what kind of difference we will make. Will we make a positive difference in the lives of people and organizations we work with each day or a negative one? Our presence or absence in a situation can alter the outcome of that situation. Even if we are oblivious to our impact, the impact is still there. However, making consistently positive differences is a matter of persistent and conscious intent. This means that we enter into situations with the awareness and desire to add value to the outcome. With this mind set in place, the chances of success are increased tenfold.

> **As you embark on learning HELIX, go forward with the notion that you are about to make a positive difference in your organization and the lives of the people who work there.**

The fastest way to build our portfolio of knowledge, skills and relationships is to share ourselves with others.

FACTOR # 2

THE PRINCIPLE OF VALUE-ADDED DELIVERY SYSTEMS

ORGANIZATIONS ARE VALUE-ADDED DELIVERY SYSTEMS

HELIX views organizations as Value-added Delivery Systems (VADS). VADS are the processes that, by intent provide a specific outcome each time they are executed. By definition, these outcomes add value to an organization's stakeholders (Owners, Employees, Customers, Suppliers, Community, etc.)

> **VADS consist of people sharing information and taking action with the intent of achieving specific outcomes.**

Whether the goal is to compensate employees, deliver product to customers or comply with regulatory agencies, VADS help sustain an organization as a dynamic concern.

This is quite a departure from the traditional view of an organization. Traditionally, organizations are viewed as hierarchical structures. In reality, these hierarchical structures are arbitrary ways to delegate authority and create a chain of command. Their arbitrary nature is evidenced by the frequency in which organization's reorganize. It seems amazing that a large percentage of managers believe that reorganizing the chain of command will yield an improvement in the way business is conducted. What hierarchical structures produce are stove pipe or egg crate organizations where the control and expansion of turf often supersede adding value to stakeholders (see Figure 4-1).

Even the downsizing craze did little to resolve the problems created through the continued allegiance to a "chain of command" view of managing organizations. Sure costs were cut and people were asked to do more for less, yet long term efficiency and prolonged productivity gains where not truly realized.

> **In fact, most downsizing efforts build bigger barriers between organizational units as each tries not to be the next ones to fall prey to the cost cutting axe.**

Early on, in working with organizations, I discovered that people will do what they need to do to get the job done. I also learned that information does not respect organizational boundaries. Think about it. Do you rely on the formal communications network or your personal relationship network for information in your organization? When the pressure is on, do you do whatever it takes, or do only what your job description allows?

> **In short, hierarchically run organizations are for bureaucrats who endorse form over substance; while VADS are for process groups that want to get things done.**

Figure 4-1 — VADS vs. Traditional Organization Structure

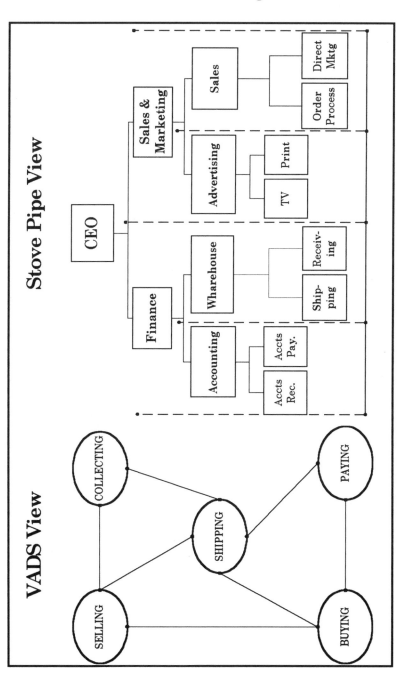

Realistically speaking there is little chance of changing the hierarchical paradigm soon. Given this reality, HELIX is designed to work with the organizational structure as-is, cultivating VADS while keeping the formal structure in place. HELIX organizes knowledge workers into focus groups using the organizations labels, culture and structure. Each focus group represents a cross section of the organization in context to a specific VADS. In this way, the chain of command is not disturbed but new informal sets of structures are created. These new structures foster cross-functional teamwork and collaboration. They help to break down defense barriers while focusing the organization on adding value to its stakeholders.

> **In essence, HELIX side steps many political land mines because it is nonthreatening to the power structure.**

When HELIX is deployed throughout an organization, it is common for the organization to evolve and restructure itself around its VADS models. There is still a chain of command, but the structure is more aligned with adding value than delegating and controlling authority.

FACTOR # 3　　　　　THE PRINCIPLE OF DISCOVERY

DISCOVERY IS CRITICAL TO LEARNING AND IMPROVEMENT

One of the key concepts within HELIX is the principle of discovery.

> **Allowing organizations and people to discover needs before defining solutions is a critical step missed by most strategic planning and business process improvement efforts**.

Discovery provides the framework for exploring the implications of change in a non threatening way. It allows teams to be creative about solutions and to develop models for improved processes that can be implemented in a practical and cost-effective manner.

Discovery is where HELIX begins. During the Discovery Phase, the needs of the business are explored. A contrast is developed between where the organization sees itself today and how it would like to see itself in the future. This future state is articulated by management by using concrete, action focused goals. When John F. Kennedy said "We will land a man on the moon by the end of this decade" he created a compelling vision for the future that was concrete and extremely focused.

These goals are linked to the key business processes of the company, its VADS. The Knowledge workers that perform these processes are organized into focus groups. Through the facilitation of these focus group teams, Value-added Delivery Systems are modeled both as they exist today and how they could exist in the future. This future state is developed in alignment with the vision set forth by management. It is during this highly interactive process that the organization begins conditioning itself for change both intellectually and emotionally. Cross-functional consensus for change emerges and momentum is built to pursue the vision. This happens because a collaborative and focused state occurs during the work session. Combining specific facilitation techniques with specific modeling techniques allows the focus group team to work on solving process issues independent of territorial concerns. In essence the process owned by the team becomes the territory, a common ground.

The beauty of HELIX's discovery process is that it takes place in a series of three short 2.5 hour work sessions. Limiting the discovery process for a specific VADS to three 2.5 hour work sessions allows participants to contribute to the improvement effort while continuing to perform their normal work efforts. The vast majority of people who participate in HELIX work sessions are overwhelmed with the creative solutions and depth of understanding that is gained in a few short hours. People become energized and talk about the experience with coworkers. True momentum is generated.

Factor # 4   The Principle of Collaboration

Breaking down barriers requires collaboration

In virtually every organization, there exists political and communication barriers that make positive change difficult, if not impossible. In order for VADS to be improved, these barriers must be neutralized or at least set aside. Fortunately, HELIX incorporates techniques that encourage collaboration. Through a structured, collaborative process, barriers are slowly dissolved. People begin to focus on process and not on each other. They become open to explore possibilities. Telling people they must cooperate, collaborate and get along with each other rarely works. More often than not people need to feel free to choose to share and collaborate. When this happens naturally, true buy-in occurs, not just compliance to the process.

> **Providing a safe environment that facilitates dialogue, and focuses on process and not individuals, allows collaboration to happen.**

While people are the mission critical component of making change happen, HELIX focuses on the process and its related work groups.

This results in reducing the risk of individuals polarizing on viewpoints, reacting defensively or withdrawing from the improvement effort. If the process focused on individuals it would concern itself with individual behaviors and performances. Doing this in groups would promote witch hunts, finger pointing and move the team away from promoting the ability of the organization to improve.

Consider the contrast between reviewing a process to discover improvements versus reviewing the individual performances related to a process. In a process focused approach the team may develop the following change concept.

In the example provided in figure 4-2 the focus is on improving the process and thus increasing the value added to customers, owners and cross functional process groups. The tone is positive and forward looking. The current situation is stated objectively without reference to fault. It sets the stage for the team to work together to develop ways to achieve the goal set forth.

Now consider the same scenario with the focus on individual performances and contributions to the process (**figure 4-3**).

In this second case it is doubtful that the representative from the order desk group is going to be supportive or collaborative. More likely, this person is going to become defensive. Defending the order desk team and getting even with the rest of the group will probably become a high priority. Improving sales order processing will probably never happen with people and performance focused approach.

Current Situation or State	Future Goal or State
The sales order process takes 2 weeks and results in poor customer service and internal stress between departments	The ability to process orders from the sales desk through shipping within 2 working days. This would improve our ability to compete more effectively, reduce the number of customer inquiries and improve working relationships between departments.

Figure 4-2 — Process Focused Change Concept

Current Situation or State	Future Goal or State
The order desk staff cannot complete sales orders correctly and sit on orders for days. These guys can't seem to get it right. Because of them, orders don't get shipped until about 2 weeks after the orders get placed. This creates a lot of stress among the rest of the departments.	The ability to get the order desk staff to do their jobs right and get orders to the warehouse fast enough for us to ship them to the customers within 2 working days.

Figure 4-3 — People Focused Change Concept

In this second case it is doubtful that the representative from the order desk group is going to be supportive or collaborative. More likely, this person is going to become defensive. Defending the order desk team and getting even with the rest of the group will probably become a high priority. Improving sales order processing will probably never happen with people and performance focused approach.

This is why focusing on the process and not individual or group performances is so critical to the HELIX approach.

People do not need to be educated on the process, nor do the collaborative and creative results to be achieved need to be promoted. The dynamics of conducting HELIX work sessions provides the framework for this to happen naturally. People may not intellectually understand what happened during the work session. They will understand that it was productive and felt right. The word will spread. Momentum will build. While learning HELIX, keep in mind that some of the techniques are designed to condition the organization to be receptive to improvement. Some people become frustrated with this part of the process because they cannot see the relationship between the effort and the physical improvements desired. Here, patience is golden.

> **To sculpt a masterpiece one needs good clay. The process of preparing the clay does not make a master sculpture. The process does enable one to work much more effectively once the sculpting begins.**

FACTOR # 5   THE PRINCIPLE OF CONTEXT

BUILDING A CONTEXT FOR DIALOGUE AND UNDERSTANDING IS ESSENTIAL

To understand the meaning of words and events, they must be viewed in their situational context. When listening to others, or viewing an exchange or set of actions without regard to their context the ability to interpret meaning and intent is lost. Words said in jest (a humorous context) are interpreted differently than those words said in anger. With political correctness all the rage today, people are being conditioned to take words and actions critically and literally without regard to their context. The result is more confrontations, hidden agendas and misaligned expectations.

The workflows that make up the VADS in an organization define the context in which people communicate and share information.

Traditionally, organizations tend to analyze processes in context to their organizational structure. While convenient and politically nonthreatening, there are rarely any demonstrable improvements achieved. More often, the barriers to cross-functional alignment, cooperation and collaboration are strengthened as people begin adopting "we versus them" attitudes.

Analyzing an organization department by department (the organizational structure) is like watching a play being performed one character at a time, independent of the plot, scenes,

31

relationships and dialogue. There would not be any CONTEXT or frame of reference for understanding the story. Consider the following lines that are taken out of context of the dialogue:

Sue: Why are you late?

Sue: Anything good?

Sue: Wow those are big ones.

Sue: You're right!

Sue: That's really a ripe banana.

John: I had to pick up a few things.

John: Yes, some lovely apples.

John: These are exceptional aren't they.

John: Thanks. If you think those are good you should taste this banana.

Without seeing the lines in their context and interaction between Sue and John it is hard to understand what is being discussed. Both Sue's and John's statements need to be read before understanding can be achieved. When reviewing an organization one department at a time, there is no context for understanding how the department's naturally work together and share information to complete processes.

Now consider this dialogue in its context.

Sue: Why are you late?

John: I had to pick up a few things.

Sue: Anything good?

John: Yes, some lovely apples.

Sue: Wow those are big ones.

John: These are exceptional aren't they.

Sue: You're right!

John: Thanks. If you think those are good you should taste this banana.

Sue: That's really a ripe banana.

Now the conversation makes sense. Clearly the conversation is about apples and bananas.

Analyzing an organization in terms of its delivery systems (its workflows) is like seeing a play or dialogue in its full CONTEXT.

HELIX allows us to understand an organization in the CONTEXT of its people and its business practices.

The next few pages explore the concept of CONTEXT and its importance to facilitating constructive dialogue and shared understanding of:

1. The organization's objectives,

2. The gap between how value is delivered today and the ideal value delivery state, and

3. The need for change and building the consensus to achieve it.

Organizational Objectives, Delivering Value and Building Consensus

How many people understand the objectives of their organization? How often are objectives viewed by the rank and file as esoteric aspirations that have little or no relevance to day-to-day operations? In your organization, can you articulate how your job supports the objectives of the company? If your answers to the above questions are:

1. Not many,
2. Most of the time, and
3. Not really

then you are not alone and this section will be of value to you.

The reason most people answer the above questions as they do is simple:

The management of many organizations do not have a clear and actionable understanding of how value is delivered to its stakeholders. They intellectually know that they are supposed to add value, they just do not know how.

Somehow, somewhere, these executives and managers have been taught that to be effective, they do not need to understand their industry at the operational level or how their business works. Instead, many believe that understanding good leadership and management techniques is all that is needed to harvest success.

With all good intention, they have isolated themselves from the day-to-day reality of delivering true value. They rely on surveys, research and a handful of advisors to keep them informed. While these are key sources of information, they mean nothing unless placed in context of how work is performed. This requires direct observation of the actual process and dialogue with those performing the work.

In short, many in management have become disconnected from the businesses they run.

Goals should be specific and concrete, not generic.

The following example from a wholesale distribution company will illustrate the disconnect that often occurs between the management that sets the objectives and the rest of the organization.

Management's Goals:

Our objective is to provide quality service to our customers.

Our objective is to have a work force that embraces excellence.

Our objective is to improve our product mix that more closely aligns with emerging market demands.

Each of these objectives while sounding good, misses the mark. What do they mean? How can they be integrated into the daily work lives of the work force who must achieve them? Let's review them one by one, take them apart and recast them in context to operational realities. The first objective states:

OUR OBJECTIVE IS TO PROVIDE QUALITY SERVICE TO OUR CUSTOMERS.

Providing quality, is always a noble pursuit. But what does it mean? Whose definition of quality will be used? How would one know if they are providing quality to customers?

 In the example of a wholesale distribution company, quality might mean the following:

1. Keeping defective merchandise returns to under 1%

2. Shipping of products within 24 hours of the time ordered

3. Processing credit applications within 2 days of receipt

These objectives become more meaningful because they begin to tie back to the act of doing. However, while their context is improved, it is not complete. The "WHAT" has been clearly stated. But the "WHY" is conspicuously missing. When objectives incorporate both "WHAT" and "WHY," they are more understandable, meaningful and achievable by the work force. The objective becomes a whole message with context.

Taking another pass at the above objectives to add "WHY," these objectives might look like this:

1. Our objective is to become the highest quality product provider in the industry by reducing defective

merchandise returns from 5 units a day to under 2 units a day.

2. Our objective is to create a new standard of speedy delivery by improving our shipping of products from 3 days to within 24 hours of the time ordered.

3. Our objective is to become the easiest company to do business with by improving the processing of credit applications from 1 week to within 2 days of receipt.

Given these three objectives, now ask the questions started in the beginning of this section:

1. Is the objective understood?

2. Can the objective be related to day-to-day operations?

3. Can the objective be related to specific job tasks like product selection, shipping, or credit review?

Just imagine if organizations would deliver these types of objectives to their work forces. Such objectives become challenges that evoke the "How To — Can Do" aspirations in people.

Clear, quantifiable, whole-message objectives become real to people.

They are direct and tangible.

They do not require dependence on surveys and other costly systems to measure and monitor.

Their achievement can be observed naturally in the outcomes produced.

The remaining examples should help drive this concept home.

Our objective is to have a work force that embraces excellence.

Who does not want to embrace excellence? Again, this objective is missing context and definition. The objective implies that the work force does not already embrace excellence. Certainly that would never be the intent of management. What this objective needs is a definition for what would constitute the embracing of excellence. This requires the company to commit itself to what it currently would believe achieving excellence would look like in action. Perhaps excellence is achieving the three objectives listed above. For a company that prides itself on its work ethic, maybe excellence is getting to work an hour early and leaving an hour late with no additional pay. Are you beginning to see how such objectives are intangible and not actionable?

For an objective to be substantive and achievable, it must be stated in context to how work is done. It must be easily understood in terms of what would constitute success.

Our objective is to improve our product mix so it more closely aligns with emerging market demands.

If this sounds like MEDIA SPEAK, it is. The questions that come to mind here are:

1. How would one know when they are closely aligned?

2. How does one measure emerging market demands?

3. What is wrong with the current product mix that it needs aligning?

Obviously, the drafter of this objective must see a need for improvement. So why not just state the improvement expectation? Consider this objective as an alternative:

> **OUR OBJECTIVE IS TO RESPOND TO OUR CUSTOMERS' DESIRE FOR CARS THAT GET 30 M.P.G. BY DEVELOPING A NEW LINE OF MID-SIZED CARS THAT MEET OR EXCEED THEIR MILEAGE EXPECTATIONS BY THE YEAR 2005.**

See the difference? Here the objective sets the bar. It clearly states the vision and presents the challenge.

How do your organization's objectives measure up? As an exercise, put together a small task force to review the organization's objectives for the coming year. They should be presented in next year's business plan. Gather the team and schedule a work session to review each objective. Using a flip chart, facilitate the group toward drafting objectives that they believe have context, challenge and measurability.

Here are the steps to follow:

1. Use one page of flip chart paper for each objective.

2. Create two columns on each page.

3. Label column one "Current Objective."

4. Label column two "Proposed Objective."

5. Write each current objective on the flip chart (This can be done in advance).

6. For each objective, have the group discuss and answer the following questions

- What operational areas of the organization does the objective relate to?

- What improvement is the objective trying to make?

- How would this improvement add value to stakeholders? Who are they?

- How would these stakeholders discern this as added value?

- How would that improvement manifest itself operationally?

- How could the improvement be measured?

- What processes does this objective impact?

- Which process groups are involved in these processes?

7. Under the current objective, write down the answers.

8. Now, have the group draft a new objective(s) that provides context, challenge and measurability based on the knowledge and consensus gained in step 6.

Congratulations! You have taken the first step toward aligning process improvement opportunities with the organization's business objectives. Now the fun begins.

For each objective, schedule a work session. Invite a key member from executive management, who has a stake in the objective. Also invite a knowledgeable representative from each of the process groups affected by the objective. The primary goal of this work session will be to fine-tune the proposed objective and gain executive and grass roots support for its achievement. The secondary goal is to begin the process of driving the objective down to the process group level. This will set the stage for work sessions that encourage a dialogue on how the related processes can be improved and objective achieved. Figure 4-4 summarizes the process of driving objectives to the VADS level.

Figure 4-4 — Driving Objectives to VADS Level

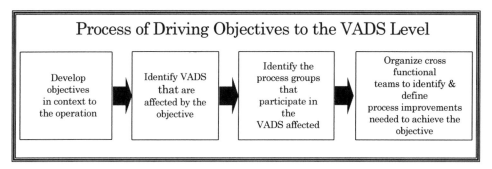

This might be thought of as risky business. What if management and operational staff cannot agree? What if things get out of hand? Relax, it's not risky. It is just the feeling of uneasiness that accompanies trying something new. Remember, do not try to sell the proposed objective. Rather, simply present the results of the task force's efforts and seek feedback. Be ready and willing to completely discard the task force's efforts in favor of alternatives that evolve from this joint work session. Treat the proposed objective as a "straw dog." Do not defend it. Just present it and let the group sculpt it. Through this process, consensus and buy-in will happen naturally. If done correctly, the task force members will be seen as action-oriented team players who are insightful and flexible.

If the review of the organization's objectives cannot be done, try reviewing a division's, a department's, a process group's or even personal objectives.

The key here is to start applying this concept and begin understanding its power to create the context and creative tension for change.

FACTOR # 6

THE PRINCIPLE OF CONDITIONING FOR CHANGE

UNCONDITIONED CHANGE CREATES RESISTANCE AND CHAOS.

Change is inevitable. People grow older and in the process change. Mountains change shape and rivers direction over millions of years. These types of changes are slow and easy to adjust to. Too much change, done too quickly creates upheaval. People can have radical reactions. Mountains can soar or crumble. Rivers can overflow or dry up. Abrupt or rapid change can throw a system out of control and into chaos.

The natural response to change is resistance.

> **Resistance to change is not good or bad, resistance to change is natural.**

People and organizations prefer to stay in a predictable and stable state. When change occurs to an organism, that organism will make internal adjustments to keep change to a minimum. It will try to keep a sense of balance and reject forces that cause stress. Science calls this state homeostasis, the self regulating of life processes.

An example will help illustrate what happens when change is encountered. Assume you begin an exercise program to get in shape. When starting an exercise program and your heart beats faster and you run out of breath, your body's natural reaction is to stop. This response to exercise is the result of your body feeling out of balance or in disequilibrium. The body wants to maintain equilibrium in context to its normal mode of operation. In response to exertion, the body has a homeostatic response. It wants to return to its comfort zone, a regular heart beat and normal breathing. This is where most exercise programs end. However, if you start slowly and continue to exercise over time, your body will begin to treat exercise as NORMAL. In fact, if you exercise at the same time everyday, your body will begin to expect the process. When you skip exercise, you will experience a homeostatic reaction that moves you toward exercising.

So the key to achieving change is persistence over time. So how does this apply to organizations?

Think of the organization as a body. When things feel smooth, they are running in a homeostatic mode — the mode in which the organization is most comfortable. If the organization feels uncomfortable, then change is afoot. If the change is dramatic enough, resistance will be visibly high. Typically morale will be low, turnover high and stress unbearable. When this type of change is caused by an outside force, a bad economy, national crisis, etc., people tend to rally together and fight their way back to normalcy. They find a common denominator and bond. However, when the change is voluntarily pursued or imposed from within the organization, heals dig in, walls go up and battle lines are drawn.

When an organization finds that change is needed to prolong its well-being, it typically pursues this change in a way that evokes the latter response. How then, can an organization pursue the radical type of change that is associated with re-engineering or major directional shifts without encountering resistance?

There is no easy answer to this. However when radical change is on the horizon, homeostatic reactions must be kept to a minimum. The organization can choose to condition the environment and people so they will be ready for it. Just like beginning an exercise program, organizations need to start slowly and build up to the change. People need time to integrate the new state of being emotionally and physically.

> **Conditioning for change need not take a great deal of time, but it does need to happen if change is to be positive and long-lasting.**

During the conditioning stage of change, it is critical that equilibrium be maintained. This means that events and situations that might invoke a homeostatic reaction must be kept to a minimum.

> **When consciously conditioning for a big change, people and organizations cannot afford to be distracted by stimuli that undermine their focus.**
>
> **They can afford distractions that act as counterbalances to the changes being brought on by the conditioning process.**

These counter balances are events or stimuli that reinforce the idea that the change being pursued is GOOD. Social functions and celebrations of minor successes are typical counterbalances that tend to work.

While conditioning (getting ready) for change, the organization must maintain equilibrium. Figure 4-5 provides illustrates this principle.

Imagine a cocktail server carrying a round tray full of drinks. To balance the tray, the server must place the drinks so as to keep the tray from tipping over. In doing this, the server must consider that the tray must stay in balance while in motion (carrying the drinks from the bar to the customers). In essence, the server has created a 360 degree lever that must remain in equilibrium during the process of delivering value (drinks) to customers. To complicate matters, the server must also understand how to remove drinks from the tray, without dumping the tray in the customer's lap (the opposite of adding value). The server will have successfully completed a cycle of adding value to customers when the tray is empty and no drinks were spilt. Therefore in going from a full tray (current state of equilibrium) to an empty tray (the changed state), the server must maintain the tray's (the organization's) equilibrium throughout the process.

This is a great metaphor and easy to visualize. It is also an effective exercise to use when training people about change. It is fun and instructive. People learn a great deal about change, chaos and equilibrium as they go from empty tray, to full tray, to tray in motion and back to empty tray. One word of caution, however. Be sure to use plastic glasses and do it outdoors. Things will get wet.

Sealed cans may also be used to avoid messes.

Figure 4-5 — Importance of Equilibrium

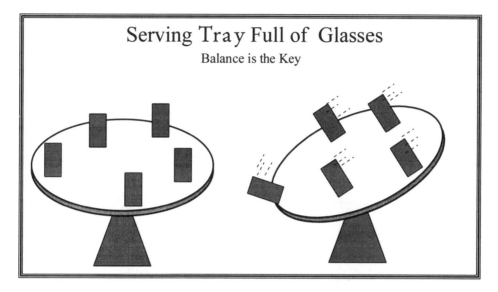

In summary, remember the following points:

1. Change will always be with us.

2. Change is a constant.

3. Rapid, unconditioned change causes resistance and chaos.

4. Change that is properly conditioned can happen quickly and relatively painlessly.

HELIX provides the conditioning processes needed to allow change to become integrated into the routine of day-to-day activity.

Since change creates chaos, it is critical that people build sufficient emotional leverage for change — if such change is to be effective and long-lasting.

PART OF THE LEVERAGE–BUILDING
PROCESS FOR CHANGE REQUIRES THAT
PEOPLE BE ALLOWED TO VENT THEIR
FRUSTRATIONS IN A NONTHREATENING,
CONSTRUCTIVE ENVIRONMENT.

Factor # 7   The Principle of Catharsis and Revelation

Catharsis and Revelation are keys to creative solutions.

Once people air their frustrations, they are more able to openly and creatively explore alternatives. HELIX's facilitation process provides the safe haven needed for process groups to collectively release their frustrations and experience the revelations that come from creative solution development.

At the beginning of each HELIX work session, participants (knowledge workers) are facilitated to develop or update a model that lists existing situations that could be improved and what that improved situation (preliminary goal) would look like. This model is called a change analysis. The model is a simple two-column format that is easy to understand. The beauty of the model is that it allows each participant to get burning issues off their chest (emotional and functional) while focusing them to project a more desirable future state.

During this portion of the work session, the facilitator asks open-ended questions of the group. These questions are focused on issues and situations that appear to impede the VADS from adding value to stakeholders.

Each group is a composite of people who represent a VADS (a process within the organization that is intended to provide a specific value to a stakeholder). As the group discusses the question the facilitator listens. As a consensus develops on an issue the facilitator paraphrases the idea and writes it on the first column of the change analysis. This becomes the Existing Situation. For each existing situation statement, the facilitator works with the group to quantify adjectives and other non-measurable descriptor's.

After a situation is talked out and quantified, the facilitator moves to the second column of the CA. This column is labeled "Preliminary Goal." The preliminary goal is a statement that reflects the group's consensus on what the process being discussed would look like if proper value were added to stakeholders. The facilitator starts a sentence with the words "The ability to ...".

The group then works to complete and quantify the goal that is paraphrased onto the flip chart by the facilitator. Once a situation and goal statement are finished the group can easily contrast why the current situation (as they see it) is bad and the preliminary goal is good in terms of adding value to stakeholders (see Figure 4-6).

Dynamically, what has happened here is that a cross-functional process group, probably for the first time in their experience, has:

1. Mutually identified undesirable situations that impede VADS,

2. Quantified the impact of that situation,

3. Agreed upon a "preliminary goal" that would correct the situation, and

4. Quantified the benefit derived through achieving the goal.

In essence they collaborated and developed some shared visions of a future state. Within a matter of 30 to 45 minutes, this cross functional process group worked together to establish objectives that the group collectively support. They have begun the emotional buy-in process needed to achieve change.

Through change analysis, a group can quickly get issues on the table. When constructing a "current situation" statement, it is okay to lament and console each other on how bad and intolerable the situation is. The facilitator encourages this catharsis. The more the group dislikes the situation, the easier it will be to change in the future. As people share their frustrations and insights a bond is formed. Inevitably they learn that they are not alone. They begin to open up. Get things on the table and where appropriate, see the humor in it all. They gain perspective, build momentum and get the leverage needed to pursue change.

As the group moves to the "preliminary goal" column they find it easy to switch gears and focus on developing a goal that resolves the situation that they just beat to death a moment earlier. It is here the creative juices of the group begin to flow.

Dialogue becomes fluid. The stage is set and the task clear. The group feels compelled to come up with a NEW WAY of doing. They jointly craft a goal that not only neutralizes the situation, but replaces it with an objective that can be easily observed and thus measured in operation.

Figure 4-6 — Change Analysis Example # 1

Change Analysis

Current Situation	Preliminary Goal

1. It takes 3 days for a sales order to get from credit to the warehouse:
 	
  – Competition averages 2 days.
  – Main reason customers complain and leave.
	1. The ability to get orders to warehouse within 6 hours of placement:
	
	  – Would undercut competition by at least 1 day.
	  – Would require streamlining of order processing through credit.

2. 30% of first-time customer quotations under $200 are never turned into orders:
 	
  – New customers cannot wait for credit approval (takes 2 weeks).
  – Competition approves in 24 hours.
  – Lose up to 300 orders & new customers a month.
	2. The ability to authorize credit limits up to $200 over the phone for first-time customers:
	
	  – Would increase sales $60,000 a month with minimal bad debt risk.
	  – Would require streamlining of order processing to handle increase in volume.

An entire section will be spent on change analysis in the implementer's guide.

> **The point to remember is that the first steps toward getting leverage on change are to release frustration, build perspective and focus on the future not the past.**

With leverage comes the creative tension (a force that pulls us forward) needed to move forward and achieve desired outcomes.

QUALITY IS THE RESULT

OF INSPIRED FOCUS

FACTOR # 8

THE PRINCIPLE OF FOCUSED URGENCY AND MOMENTUM

FOCUSED URGENCY IS KEY TO MAINTAINING MOMENTUM

Urgency is often associated with reacting to what appears to be the most pressing issue at the time. This is often referred to as the "Tyranny of the Urgent." In this context urgency is not considered a good thing. However, there is another form of urgency that helps people and organizations achieve results; focused urgency. Focused urgency is the process of acting with deliberate dispatch on goals that are important. Focused urgency rivets attention on what is important while screening out interference and distraction. Through focused urgency an organization or person accelerates the pace of their actions until the desired result is achieved.

When an organization sets out to achieve objectives, it is critical that they do so with focused urgency. In doing so energy and momentum are maintained. People see the objective as a serious and passionate pursuit of the organization. Focused urgency builds shared vision and direction.

Virtually all high achievers instinctively understand the importance of focused urgency. They know how to become single minded in their actions.

Without focused urgency, it is doubtful that any form of major initiative will succeed. Consider what happened to the Republican Party's Contract with America in 1996. Try to set a side any political affinities and focus on what happened without any value judgments of Good or Bad. Initially, the party demonstrated almost perfect focused urgency.

The House and Senate acted on the contract without regard to the distractions and pressures of the opposition or the media. Despite the complaints made through the media, the approval rating in the polls was high. Then, the focus was lost. The more conservative elements in the Senate began to get nervous. They began to question the pace of change and fell prey to the old paradigm of back-room politics and compromise. The result, disaster for the party.

The lynch pin to the downward spiral in the party's approval ratings began when the battle over the budget began. The Republicans were willing to let the government suffer a temporary shutdown rather than perpetuate more and more deficit spending. The Democrats saw this as their last stand and applied tremendous pressure through the media. The cries of impending doom and personal financial ruin for loyal Federal employees, the aged and disadvantaged dominated the media. The threats of not issuing needed Social Security checks and cutting off the needy from welfare proved too much for the old-line Senate Republicans and the momentum was lost never to return.

What happened was the Democratic Party was able to expend a greater level of focused urgency than the Republicans. They were able to sustain momentum where the Republicans could not.

56

> **Organizations that harness the power of focused urgency set the pace for others to follow.**

Each action builds on the last. Objectives become rallying points. There is no confusion or doubt as to the path the group is taking or what will be accomplished.

CHAPTER SUMMARY

In this chapter, 8 key factors were presented which form the philosophical foundation of HELIX. HELIX is as much a philosophy as it is a set of pragmatic tools and techniques for helping organizations discover ways to improve processes and achieve alignment.

Through the **Principle of Making a Difference** an organization can instill a positive attitude for moving forward.

The **Principle of Value-added Delivery Systems** helps the organization move away from viewing itself as a hierarchy to viewing itself as a series of cross functional activities that add value to its stakeholders.

The **Principle of Discovery** frees the organization to explore and to tap into its human resources for ways to improve how it adds value to stakeholders.

The **Principle of Collaboration** provides the understanding that breakthrough learning and growth comes through dialogue and collaboration during periods of discovery.

The **Principle of Context** presents how to energize collaborative work efforts by creating meaningful objectives that are actionable at all levels of the organization.

The **Principle of Conditioning for Change** provides insights into how people and organizations react to change. The process of conditioning people and organizations for change, if change is going to be successful, is introduced.

The **Principle of Catharsis and Revelation** explores the human need to vent before they can let go and move forward and unleash their creativity. It provides a stable and non confrontational method of allowing people to achieve this process.

The **Principle of Focused Urgency and Momentum** presents how an organization can achieve its objectives without becoming reactive.

These 8 key factors represent the bedrock upon which HELIX is based

QUESTIONS TO REFLECT ON

Each chapter in the book concludes with a series of questions to consider and reflect on. The intent is to provide a series of questions that will allow for an assessment of the concepts presented in context to how you perceive your organization and yourself within in it.

1. What difference will your Organization make today? What difference will you make?

2. What are 5 of your organization's Value-added Delivery Systems? Which process groups are involved in those systems?

3. How much time does your organization spend on

discovering how it adds value? How much time do you spend?

4. What approach does your organization use to pursue discovering process improvement opportunities? Who is involved in the process?

5. How does your company foster cross functional collaborative and open dialogue?

6. How actionable are your organization's business objectives?

7. How does your organization know when it is delivering value to its stakeholders? How do you know?

8. How real are the organization's objectives to front line workers?

9. How do front line workers know if their day-to-day actions are supporting the organization's goals and objectives? How does top management know? How do you know?

10. How well do your organization's objectives clearly state what is to be achieved, why it needs to be achieved and how that achievement will be measured?

11. What changes have been resisted within your organization? What changes have been embraced?

12. What are some of the factors that have lead to resisting change in the organization? What are some of the factors that have lead to embracing change?

13. How does your organization condition itself and employees for change?

14. How does your organization help its people to unleash their creativity?

15. How are creative thinking and problem solving embraced in practice within your organization?

16. How does your organization focus itself to achieve objectives? How do you?

Take the time needed to write down your thinking and reflections related to the above questions. Use a change analysis format to capture how you answered the questions now (current situation) and how you would have liked to have answered the questions (preliminary goal). Finally, facilitate a group of your peers through the questions in a change analysis session. See if you can vent frustrations and tap into some creative thinking around ways to achieve any preliminary goals that are developed.

Knowledge Workers are
Consciously aware of their impact
on the process.

CHAPTER 5   THE ALIGNMENT FACTORS

ENSURING INTERIM DESTINATION POINTS CONNECT

Before launching into an orientation on the actual tools and techniques of HELIX, there are a few concepts that need to be reviewed. Each of the concepts presented here is important to factor into the HELIX process. Understanding, defining and aligning an organization to its stakeholder's needs and expectations is the reason business process improvement (continuous or re-engineering), TQM and yes, HELIX exist. Figure 5-1 depicts each of the interim destination points that when factored together help organizations to achieve total alignment.

Once these factors are understood, building, diagnosing and working with HELIX tools and techniques will be become a natural extension of the process.

Figure 5-1 — Key Alignment Factors

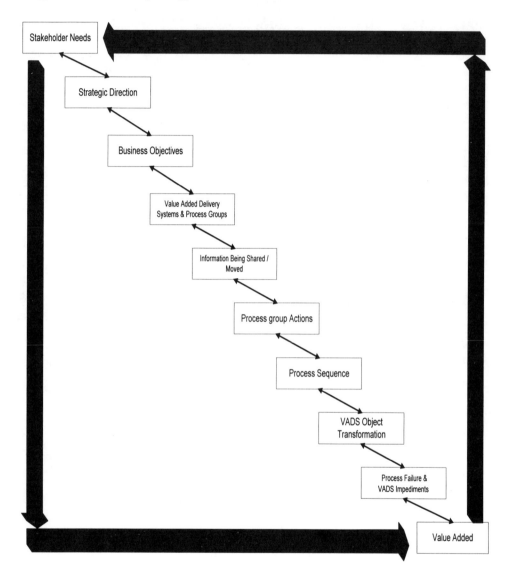

FACTOR # 9   **ALIGNMENT OF STAKEHOLDER NEEDS TO STRATEGIC DIRECTION**

Aligning stakeholder needs to strategic direction requires that: 1) the organization knows who its stakeholders are and what they want; 2) the organization has a consciously developed strategic direction. All organizations have stakeholders and a direction being followed. The distinction is whether or not the organization is consciously aware of either.

Organizations exist to satisfy stakeholder needs for value. Typically, these stakeholders are:

1. Owners

2. Customers

3. Employees

4. Community and

5. Strategic Alliances and Providers

Logically speaking, to consciously add value to a stakeholder, there must be an understanding of what that value should be. In short, what are the stakeholder's expectations? To understand wants and expectations, an organization needs to listen to stakeholders. This listening process includes dialogue as well as observation of actions. Surveys, market research and competitive analysis are typical tools used to understand and define stakeholder needs and expectations. However direct observation and dialogue are better tools. Even though these latter techniques take more time to use they produce far more profound understanding.

If an organization does not understand its stakeholder's needs, then it is unlikely that it will align those needs with its strategic direction. Of course this assumes that the organization has a strategic direction. All organizations have a direction being pursued. The question is whether or not the organization is aware and in control of that direction and whether it is strategic in nature or not. This is not a trivial issue. Most organizations can be likened to a ship on the ocean. Some have a clear objective in mind and a deliberate plan to navigate toward an objective. Most others merely float along at the mercy of the winds and currents that they encounter along the way to wherever destination they might find.

Imagine getting on an airplane that had no predefined destination. Would you do it? You might if you were adventurous, had a parachute and time to kill. However most people would not. Yet, everyday, thousands of people get on board the 'Organization Express' to nowhere.

Fortunately, the absence of understanding stakeholders and strategic direction does not render HELIX useless it just means it cannot be deployed strategically.

> **Often, deploying HELIX at any level increases the chance that people will begin to think more strategically.**

For now, assume that the organization understands its stakeholder needs and has a business plan that sets forth its strategic direction and business objectives. Does this mean that the strategy is consciously aligned with stakeholder needs? If the business plan explicitly correlates strategy to stakeholder needs then the answer is yes. If it does not, then more likely than not, the answer is no.

Why is it so important to align stakeholder needs to strategic direction?

Simply stated, it is important to ensure the long-term success of the organization.

Tom Vogl, one of my colleagues, often encourages me to write a book called "The Death of a Corporation". In the over 10 years we have worked together, Tom and I have seen the leaders of multiple organizations do many unexplainable things — as if their goal was failure. They write policies that prevent rather than enable. They rationalize their decisions with facts after emotionally based decisions are made. They think money first and results second. The list goes on and on. Generally, however, these leaders are doing the best they can. What they are missing is a clear understanding of how to better the lives of their organization's internal and external stakeholders.

Once the organization understands:

1. Stakeholder needs,

2. Its relative position in the market place and

3. Its aspirations to be achieved (where it wants to be as opposed to where it is now),

developing an aligned strategic direction is not all that difficult.

> **Once the needs and direction are established and communicated throughout the organization, a context for evaluating process improvement opportunities is created.**
>
> **This context becomes the driving force behind building meaningful and achievable business objectives.**

FACTOR # 10 ALIGNMENT OF STRATEGIC DIRECTION TO BUSINESS OBJECTIVES

Once a strategic direction has been established (a path that moves the organization toward a greater fulfillment of stakeholders' needs), it needs to align its business objectives to that direction. In essence once the company has defined WHO (stakeholders) it serves and WHERE (strategic direction) it wants to go, it needs to build a series of WHATS (business objectives) that will get them to the WHERE.

Business objectives should be stated in context to the strategic direction they support. This way, there can be no doubt why the business objective is important.

Remember, good business objectives are specific enough to leave nothing to interpretation.

Good objectives contain the criteria for knowing when success has been achieved and plainly states the challenge.

Consider the objective statement:

OUR OBJECTIVE IS TO PROVIDE QUALITY SERVICE TO OUR CUSTOMERS.

In the above statement the phrase "Quality service" is too vague. How would the rank and file know if quality service was being provided? What does it look like in action or outcome?

Now consider the following statement as an alternative to the one above.

> **OUR OBJECTIVE IS TO BECOME THE HIGHEST QUALITY PRODUCT PROVIDER IN THE INDUSTRY BY REDUCING DEFECTIVE MERCHANDISE RETURNS FROM 5 TO LESS THAN 1 PER DAY.**

Notice how quality is defined in terms of reducing returns from 5 to less than one per day. This simple measurement provided within the objective allows everyone to understand what success would look like.

Below are two more examples of meaningful and actionable objective statements.

> **OUR OBJECTIVE IS TO CREATE A NEW STANDARD OF SPEEDY DELIVERY BY IMPROVING OUR SHIPPING OF PRODUCTS FROM 3 DAYS TO WITHIN 24 HOURS OF THE TIME ORDERED.**

Again, the definition of speedy delivery is defined.

> **OUR OBJECTIVE IS TO BECOME THE EASIEST COMPANY TO DO BUSINESS WITH BY IMPROVING THE PROCESSING OF CREDIT APPLICATIONS FROM 1 WEEK TO WITHIN 2 DAYS OF RECEIPT.**

Getting the idea?

The basic concept is to develop objectives that identify WHAT is to be achieved and HOW success of that achievement will be measured. Remember that the measurement should be

70

understandable by everyone and be easy to observe in action.

A real-life example will help to drive this point home.

During the writing of this book, a nationally known retail giant is rumored to be on the verge of bankruptcy. The other morning the story on this company's plight was broadcast on a cable news network. The story had two segments. The first was an interview with a customer who was just coming out of the store. The second segment was on the company's strategy for maintaining its number two market position. In this example, assume that all the facts about the situation were disclosed in the news story. In reality, the company is most likely deploying a multifaceted strategy to maintain its market position.

The customer was asked if she shops at the store a lot at Christmas and, if not, why not. Her response was simple; "No. "

1. They do not carry a full line of toys.

2. The people are not very friendly.

3. The service is terrible (she cited her experience of it taking 20 minutes to return an item).

In the interview with a company representative they indicated that the company's strategic direction is to maintain or improve its current position in the retail industry. Their supporting action (objective) was to hire another national chain's key executive who will aggressively re-merchandise the company's lines and implement more entertaining TV commercials.

Certainly, re-merchandising might resolve the toy selection issue, although that is not explicit in the objective. Clever advertising might generate new trial visits from customers. However, if they are confronted with poor selection, unfriendly people and poor service, that improvement will be short-lived.

So, not to be a thrower of rocks without an alternative, what might the company be doing instead?

First, it could have hired the customer just interviewed. In three short statements she put her finger on the pulse of the dilemma. Poor selection, unfriendly people and poor service. Who of us shoppers have braved the dreaded price check and wished we had scheduled a root canal instead.

Clearly, in this example, there is a disconnect between what customers want and business objectives (actions needed to achieve the strategy).

After listening to the customer and cringing at the company's new approach to solving its problems, my mind raced with an approach it might take instead.

Here are some thoughts:

1. Solving the selection problem will take time and research. Besides, most people go to this store with specific purchases in mind. Here, a campaign should be started to learn what the customer did not find while they were shopping. This would be done at each store by courteous professionals who would have dialogues with customers on a random basis. Each customer spoken with would receive a promotional discount coupon good on any product store wide during their next month's visit. The objective could be stated as follows:

"In our efforts to provide our customers with the right selection of products, we will conduct an "at the store" research campaign to determine what the customer expected to find and then adjust our product mix to reflect customer demand."

The approach outlined accomplishes a number of things:

- Customer feedback is achieved at the point where service is provided.

- Customers are rewarded for their participation making them feel listened to and good about the experience.

- The reward provided (discount coupon good for next visit), will help drive repeat visitations.

2. Solving the friendliness and service problems can be done quickly and would go a long way toward changing people's impression of the store as a place to shop. Here, a blitz of all stores would take place. For 30 minutes before and after every shift, employees would be gathered to receive training on customer service and to conduct a change analysis session on what needs to improve in order to provide friendlier, more efficient service to customers.

Customers would be invited on occasion to provide feedback directly to frontline staff at these sessions. Ideas and concepts would be shared with all stores. Stores exhibiting the most improvement would get incentive awards (bonuses for employees). Once evidence of improvement was observed in enough stores, a new campaign would ensue touting the stores as the friendly, easy place to shop. The objective could read as follows:

"To provide our customers with friendlier staff and faster service, we will conduct a complete retraining of all our frontline employees.

To demonstrate our commitment to this improvement, we will create an incentive program that will reward stores that achieve the greatest improvement over the next 12 months. Our improvements will be determined by our sales volumes and customer responses to "at the store" interviews."

Although these objectives would not qualify for the "cute sound bite award," they do provide a clear picture of what is going to happen and why it is needed. Too many times, business objectives are written to appeal to the board of directors and top management.

> **Business objectives need to be written to appeal to those who will carry out the work.**

The day-to-day line workers need objectives that they can understand, embrace and pursue. Without the physical and emotional support of the line workers, most objectives become nothing more than a set of esoteric phrases that tickle the intellectual fancy of corporate aristocracy.

> **Real alignment within an organization happens when top management provides a strategic direction that is supported by business objectives that rally and compel the workforce to action.**

FACTOR # 11   **ALIGNMENT OF BUSINESS OBJECTIVES TO VALUE-ADDED DELIVERY SYSTEMS AND PROCESS GROUPS**

Now that there are business objectives that support both the strategic direction and stakeholder needs, how do those objectives manifest themselves in operation? A few pages back the concept of Value-added Delivery Systems was presented. To review, Value-added Delivery Systems (VADS), represent processes that provide stakeholders with expected value. They are workflows that have the conscious intent to provide specific products and services to the stakeholders of an organization. Examples include:

1. **The process of selling** (from point of order through delivery and payment) Here the stakeholders are the customer (receiving value for money), and the owners or stockholders (making a profit on the sale).

2. **The process of compensating employees** (from beginning of a pay period through pay check distribution): Here the stakeholders are the employee (receiving money for services provided), and the employer (receiving labor or value for money).

3. **The process of divisional business planning** (from reviewing the organization's strategy & business objectives to assessing last years performance, to developing divisional objectives and action plans to creating budgets and to getting approval): Here the stakeholders are everyone

connected to the organization (customers, employees, owners, vendors and community).

In each of these examples, the VADS encompasses many transactions and process groups. In the case of the sales process, those process groups might include the:

1. Order desk (people who take the order)

2. Credit (people who verify that the customer is credit worthy)

3. Shipping (people who deliver the product)

4. Billing (people who bill for the product that was ordered and shipped)

5. Collections (people who post the payment to the order completing the sales cycle).

So how does one align the objectives of the business with VADS? This is where the true test of quality business objectives lies. Here is where even the best upwardly aligned business objectives breakdown. To use a football analogy, the play book is great, but execution is where it's at. It is through VADS that objectives are executed. If the objectives are missing at the VADS level, there is little chance for continued success. To achieve this level of alignment, there needs to be a conscious and deliberate effort. Once the business objectives are established, they need to be correlated with each of the VADS that will support them.

> **For each VADS identified, a team that represents the knowledge needed to perform the VADS is formed.**
>
> **This team is made up of line employees who perform the actions needed to complete the VADS processes**

> **The team's objective will be to expand on the company's business objectives in terms of the operational changes needed to ensure success.**

This critical step in the business planning process is virtually never done. Instead, organizations distribute their strategies and objectives to operating divisions and departments. These groups then work in virtual vacuums to build their portion of the business plan. What appears to be a logical "top down" process is actually illogical. There is no assurance that these lower-level plans are coordinated or even support the VADS that drive the organization's success.

The more logical approach would be to generate the second level of the business plan via VADS teams. VADS teams would review how their processes and communications are impacted (explicitly or implicitly) by the business objectives. Since each team would have developed VADS objectives that align with the business objectives, each department represented would be able to identify which of those objectives impacted their department in terms of how work is performed.

For instance, if the purchasing department had work roles in three VADS then it would participate in three VADS teams. The staff could review those three VADS business plans and extract their portion of involvement in context to the value being added. Around this information that they helped to create, via their participation on the three teams, purchasing could develop a departmental plan. This plan would include the training and administrative requirements needed to support the business objectives in context to the VADS. The purchasing department could then develop departmental objectives and programs that clearly support the organization's business objectives and the VADS that are impacted. Instead of working in departmental funnels, the department works in collaborative cross functional teams.

This improves alignment and rapport throughout the organization. This is how alignment is assured and business objectives migrated to supporting departmental objectives. It is also how VADS improvement opportunities are discovered as part of an ongoing planning process.

This process takes no more time to accomplish than the traditional approach. It does, however, require a shift in the paradigm away from the stove pipe organization toward a cross functional collaborative one.

Clearly, typical organizations do not operate in context to their organizational structures. In many ways, organizations should take a lesson from football teams. Football teams are organized around the way the game is played. There is an offensive team, defensive team and special team. This works because only one team is on the field at a time. Since each team is cross functional in nature (throwers, runners, catchers and blockers) there is a natural environment for communication that is critical to the goal of winning the game.

Each team has a specific value they add to the game. The offense is to score points. The defense is to prevent the other team's offense from scoring points and special teams handle special projects like punt returns. Each team has its play book. However, reflect a moment on what a football game might be like if teams were organized the way organizations are. Instead of an offense, defense and special team units, there would be a Linemen Department, Runner Department, Thrower Department, Catcher Department and Kicker Department. Each department would have staff that played on various teams. Some would play on offense, some defense and others on special teams. Each department would receive the strategy from the head coach (win the game). Each would develop its objectives and action plans for the game. Each would have the same play book to work from (business plan).

The only difference would be that each department would call its own play for any given down, just the way departments often work without regard to other departments. The result would be chaos. For instance, in a given play, the lineman may push the opposing team's line right while the runners decide that going left is the best idea. Meanwhile the catchers decide to run a short post pattern and the throwers decide to throw the bomb. The only predictable outcome is that the thrower (quarterback) will get sacked and the team thrown for a loss.

But this does not happen that way in football. Instead, each VADS team (offense, defense, etc.) huddle before each down to agree upon a play (they share information and expectations). The coach (CEO) and quarterback (team leader) also meet every 4 plays or so to collaborate on what should happen during the next set of plays.

The game plan (business plan) is dynamic and is continually adjusted based on the score, the other team's strategy and each team's observable strengths and weaknesses. Offensive and defensive (competitive intelligence) coaches observe the game from high in the stadium so they can see the big picture. They are in constant, real-time, communication with the head coach who can use this information to better guide the team. Everything is aligned and coordinated **(see Figure 5-2)**.

Today's organizations seem to discourage communication and collaboration in real time. Despite management's desires and words, their actions often indicate they are more concerned with financial controls and protocol than with winning the game. Territories and turf are preserved at all cost. Team performances are almost never reviewed in context to VADS. Business and departmental plans are communicated through a series of baton passes without dialogue with the frontline employees whose actions ultimately determine the success or failure of the plan.

Take a moment to personalize what you have just read. In your organization, how many times have you felt that there is a communication problem? Statements like "The right hand does not know what the left hand is doing" or "No one communicates around here" or "I feel like a mushroom, left in the dark and fed ...."

Figure 5-2 — VADS vs. Stove Pipe Organizations

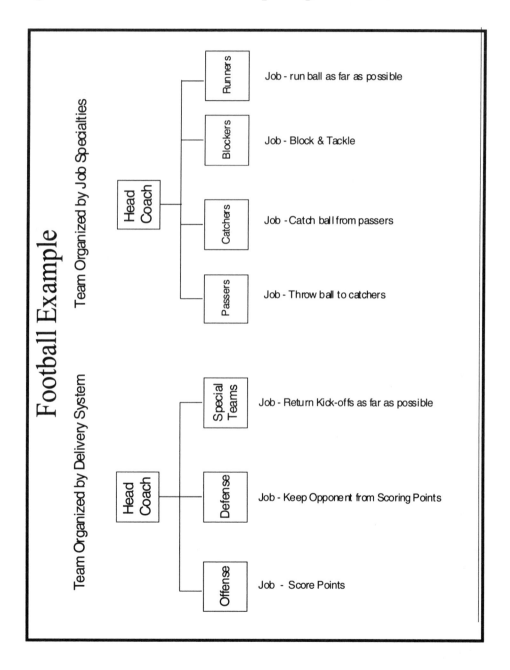

THE HELIX FACTOR

How often do these kinds of frustrations occur within your process group? How often are they targeted at process groups you interface with, or upper management? Could this be due to a disconnect between your understanding of how your day-to-day work activities align with what is important to the company? Could it be that you have trouble from time to time relating to how your daily routines add value to anyone? Do some of your work actions seem like mindless busywork, or do they seem like critical steps toward ensuring that the company is fulfilling its vision?

If you, or people you know, can relate to these feelings and frustrations, then maybe, just maybe, the old ways of pushing strategy down through the chain of command hasn't worked. Maybe a new model is needed. Maybe that new model should be VADS driven.

Consider this. As you think and reflect, observe your organization in action. Talk to people. Ask them to share with you how their job relates to supporting the business objectives. Ask them how it relates to adding value to stakeholders. Listen to your own feelings and instincts. You might be pleasantly surprised or you might be horrified.

Through HELIX comes a way to align business objectives with VADS. The HELIX process promotes this alignment explicitly and implicitly. HELIX can be deployed without changing the traditional stove pipe structures that are already in place. It allows traditional stovepipe structures and VADS structures to coexist.

FACTOR # 12   ALIGNMENT OF VALUE-ADDED DELIVERY SYSTEMS AND PROCESS GROUPS TO THE INFORMATION BEING SHARED & MOVED

What do process groups do? They share information among themselves and other process groups. This information typically relates to completing a portion of a larger effort. When the sales desk completes and sends the sales order to the credit department for approval, they are performing only a small piece of work in the sales process. The act of sending the order to the credit department implies that more work will need to be done before the order can be laid to rest. The credit department in turn adds value to the order by approving it and authorizing it for shipment. This act of sharing information to move work through the organization does not happen by accident.

It is amazing how often the people performing work have no context for what the ultimate outcome of the effort is.

They do not understand how their actions impact others and ultimately the stakeholders.

This disconnect between work action and work value is the major cause for poor quality and errors in organizations.

How does this happen? Surely, people understand their jobs and why they are important. NOT NECESSARILY. For many, a job is just a way to earn a living, nothing more. This is typically so because they do not understand their job in context to how it adds value to the organization.

You do not have to go very far in some organizations to find this. I know a number of middle managers making well over $50,000 a year who have serious questions about how their actions and those of their staff contribute to the success of the company.

They do not know the vision, the strategy or the objectives of the company. They have little or no idea how to align their actions with other groups in the organization. They feel isolated and left out of the loop. Basically, they work solely to support their families and their weekends; not for their vocational and career growth.

In 1974 I learned a lesson.

> **People need to understand their job in context to the value they create and the VADS in which they participate.**

At the time I managed a service bureau. One of my data entry operators was marginal at her job. Her error rate was about 30%, and her input speed was about 2,000 keystrokes an hour (average would be about 4,000). Counseling was not working. One day, in a last ditch effort to salvage her position, we had a conversation about the impact her work had on our clients and our ability to be successful. Her primary job was to enter payroll transactions so they could be processed and checks produced. She was a good person and I could not accept that her work performance was due to lack of caring. I explained that when she made errors, people's paychecks were wrong.

This in turn inconvenienced these people and reflected poorly on our client relationships. I then explained how her paycheck was a by-product of our clients paying us for producing accurate paychecks for their employees. Her eyes grew large. She suddenly saw how her job added value to other people. What happened next amazed me.

Over the next sixty days, her speed and accuracy improved. She began coming in early to do her work so she would have time to run printouts and balance her jobs. Within six months her hourly keystroke rate went from 2,000 to over 9,000. When I shared this story with the data processing manager he told me that was impossible. We both clocked her without her knowing. He was right, she was really keying at about 15,000 keystrokes an hour. That's over 4 strokes a second. You could hardly see her fingers as they danced over the keys. Her accuracy rate was about 99%.

At her review, six months later, I asked her what she attributed to the improvement. She told me two things. First, she felt important because I had taken the time to help her. She felt wanted and cared about in her job. Second, she believed that she was helping others by her job. This made her feel needed and important. She knew how important her paycheck was and could relate to how important paychecks were for the thousands of people we produced them for. She wanted to do a good job so that the company could continue to get more clients and she could help more people get paid.

I was speechless. At 24 years old, and just trying to avoid the unpleasant job of firing someone, I learned that spending time with a person to educate them on how their job fit into a broader picture was critical to producing quality output and job satisfaction.

Who do you know that fits this description? How many people in your organization could benefit from understanding their job in context to the value it provides to stakeholders?

These same people, once they have been allowed to view their jobs in context to the VADS they support, often become energized and self-directed. For the first time they can see their efforts in context to a greater effort (delivering value). They become creative contributors to the process.

> **Aligning and understanding how and why process groups share information sets the stage for breakthrough process improvements.**

FACTOR # 13   ALIGNMENT OF INFORMATION BEING SHARED TO STIMULUS TRIGGERS AND PROCESS GROUP ACTIONS

Stimulus Triggers are the visual, audio, tactile or other sensory queues that let a person know when to take action. Within the context of HELIX a stimulus trigger alerts a knowledge worker that it is time to perform a predetermined set of actions related to information moving through a specific VADS.

In traditional work environments stimulus triggers often take the form of paperwork appearing in front of someone. However, stimulus triggers take many forms. For a hotel front desk clerk a stimulus trigger is a guest appearing at the front desk. The guest's mere appearance alerts the clerk to inquire how they can help the guest. At that point a key placed on the counter could trigger the actions needed to check the guest out of the hotel. For a firefighter, the sound of a siren triggers the actions needed to put out a fire.

Sometimes people set off triggers in others by accident. When this occurs, there is a disconnect between their expectations and the actions they observe. Body language can be misinterpreted or a poorly written memo can be misunderstood. Requests for service can be ignored.

When embarking on an effort to improve VADS related work processes, it is important to explicitly understand the stimulus triggers that will occur and the subsequent actions that are to be taken. It is also important to understand how fast action is to be taken once the trigger has occurred.

Finally, there needs to be an understanding of the frequency of these stimulus triggers within a given time frame. In short, stimulus triggers must be understood in terms of what they are, how fast action must be taken and how often they occur.

Why does all this need to be known? Aren't most stimulus triggers obvious to people that do their job day in and day out?

Not always and not by the VADS team as a whole. How many times have you stood at a service counter wanting to be helped only to be seemingly ignored by the three clerks only six feet away? Or how many times have you been in a restaurant wanting the bill and becoming frustrated when you are unable to get your server's attention? How about the paperwork that sits on someone's desk for two weeks longer than expected? Are the people doing these jobs consciously ignoring their duties? Are they incompetent? Maybe.

Most likely, they have been poorly trained in either understanding how to interpret stimulus triggers, the expected response to those triggers, or the speed of response required. It could be that they have been trained some time ago and their supervisors do not know how to properly reinforce the proper behaviors. Of course this would require the supervisor to be consciously aware of these triggers as well.

To adequately understand why VADS work the way they do and to understand how to improve them, the cause and effect relationships need to be understood at a detailed level. The people doing the job must have no doubts when to take action. People must also have a clear understanding of how fast they are expected to respond in each situation. Consciously understanding stimulus triggers in context to the VADS and the actions that enable them helps people to be better performers and contribute to the improvement process.

Understanding stimulus triggers raises the knowledge workers conscious awareness of what is going on around them in the workplace. They become more competent in their interpretation of queues. They learn how to focus on stimulus triggers and disregard distractions. Their perceptual acuity is heightened. In essence, in a field full of flowers and weeds, they are being trained to recognize the flowers while not being distracted by the weeds.

The fastest way to build our portfolio of knowledge, skills and relationships is to share ourselves with others.

FACTOR # 14 ALIGNMENT OF PROCESS GROUP ACTIONS TO PROCESS SEQUENCE

Along with understanding the stimulus triggers that queue people to take action, it is important for the VADS team to understand the order in which these actions must take place. Rework, inefficiency and failure are often the result of people taking the right actions in the wrong sequence.

In the morning most people get ready to go to work. Hopefully each of them has learned to get ready in the proper sequence. The actions of taking a shower, drying their hair and getting dressed are second nature to them. But what would happen if this sequential set of actions were not second nature to them?. How long and with what results would it take someone to get ready for work if they got up, dried their hair, got dressed and then took a shower. Hopefully, they would learn from this mistake, get dry clothes, re-dry their hair and continue on with their day. They would learn, because the feedback of standing dripping wet and fully dressed would be fairly dramatic. But what if there was no feedback? What if they did not understand the cause and effect of doing things out of sequence? They might be inclined to repeat this process over and over every day. They might get good at it and resist corrective action. Sounds farfetched doesn't it?

Consider an organization that is plagued with inventory problems because they update their inventory records for orders only after shipment has occurred. There are no flaws in the action steps, just flaws in their sequence. In this example, inventory levels are out of sync with reality since they are not updated at the point they are sold. Watch how this simple sequencing error causes dramatic problems.

To start, assume there are 5 widgets in inventory.

Customer 1 orders 3 widgets. The sales desk looks in the inventory book and sees that there are 5 widgets in stock. No problem here. The sales desk confirms the order and promises delivery in 2 days. A few minutes later, customer 2 orders 4 widgets. Since the inventory book has not been updated for the customer 1's order, there still appears to be 5 widgets in the warehouse. So another order is prepared, promises for delivery made and forwarded for shipping. At this point 7 widgets have been ordered while there are physically only 5 in stock. This process continues throughout the day.

The next day the first widgets are pulled for shipping to customer 1. The shipped order is forwarded to inventory control and the widget levels reduced. Now the fun begins. When customer 2's order is pulled for shipping, there is only two widgets. The warehouse indicates this on the order and forwards to customer service for processing.

Customer service, in turn, calls customer 2 and explains that the company is out of widgets and that it will take three weeks to fill the order. Customer 2 is not happy because they use these widgets in their production process and will now have to inform their customers that delays are in the works.

The ripple effect has begun. Meanwhile more orders are hitting the warehouse for widgets. More orders are going into back-order status. Purchasing gets thrust into the loop. Tension mounts as they are pressed to get more widgets right away to fill all the back-orders. Purchasing responds and orders more widgets to respond to this new-found demand. However, customer 8 has had enough and three days from now cancels their order for 30 widgets. No one tells purchasing which has 100 widgets on order. In a few weeks, everyone will be wondering why there are so many angry customers because of the lack of widget availability when there are so many in the warehouse.

This little scenario and others like it is not uncommon. Because of a simple sequencing errors, a set of events can be triggered that causes major reductions in service levels, morale and sales. Stakeholders suffer because the organization did not understand the cause and effect impact of a VADS that processes information in the wrong sequence.

Look into your organizations. Are there outcomes that do not make sense? Are there people doing their job (taking the actions they have been trained to take) but getting results that are replete with anomalies? If so, then there might be sequence errors in the actions being taken.

By using the HELIX workflow mapping techniques and correlating these maps back to the change analysis, action sequencing errors can be identified and engineered out of VADS.

WE MUST PERFORM

BEFORE WE PROMISE.

FACTOR # 15 ALIGNMENT OF PROCESS SEQUENCE TO VADS OBJECT TRANSFORMATIONS

To understand where action sequencing errors exist there needs to be an understanding of the relationships between process sequence and the concept of object transformation. In the context of workflows, objects are the core subject matters being moved through a process. As an object is moved from one process group to another, it changes or transforms. This means that it has different characteristics coming out of the process group than it had going into the process. These transformations manifest themselves as changes in the object's status.

In every VADS there is at least one primary object. Often there are secondary objects as well. In the earlier widget sales example the primary object is the order. Two secondary objects are the customer and inventory. As the order was processed through the organization it changed status a number of times. As the order moved from the order desk to credit it had a status of "open order pending credit approval."

At this point, the inventory and customer objects also changed. The inventory available for sale went down by the quantity of widgets ordered. The customer's credit limit also went down by the value of the order. As the order moved from credit to the warehouse, it became an "approved order." It subsequently became a shipped and then a billed order.

Typically these transformations are evidenced by physical changes to paperwork or updates to databases. In the example the error in the VADS was the failure to reduce the inventory available for a sale when the order was taken. Here is an important point that should not be over looked.

> **Objects transform whether the transformation is recognized or not.**

The reality is, there was less inventory available for sale even though the records did not reflect it.

> **One of the keys to designing effective and efficient VADS is to understand how and when objects transform as they move through a process.**

Failure to understand object transformation results in rework, reduced customer service levels, frustration and costly errors. The widget example illustrates this well.

Conversely, movements of objects between process groups that do not result in transformations are candidates for removal from the VADS. Typically this type of movement is seen when paperwork is reviewed needlessly by a manager or it is passed on by a secretary for approval. Such movements and needless handling are typically imposed on a process in an attempt to overlay controls and safeguards. More often than not, moving information through a VADS without each movement adding to the completion of that VADS makes it bureaucratic and inefficient. These types of procedures should be challenged and removed where appropriate.

FACTOR # 16   ALIGNMENT OF VADS OBJECT TRANSFORMATION TO THE VALUE-ADDED

As objects transform they should have a discernible incremental increase in value. This means that transformation of an object directly leads to the completion of the current VADS cycle or positions a future cycle for success. In the widget example, the failure to reduce the number of widgets available for sale sabotaged future orders. The sales desk, thinking it had enough inventory to satisfy the customer's need took orders and promised delivery dates that could not be fulfilled. This had a direct impact on customer relations and service levels. It also affected the work of other employees, keeping them from adding value to the process and the related stakeholders.

When engineering VADS it is imperative that each object being transformed be tested for the value that transformation has on current and future VADS cycles. Too often organizations ignore this step in their process improvement and re-engineering efforts. Understanding object transformation in context to adding value to VADS requires breaking processes down to their most fundamental level. This is a level of detail that most people would rather avoid but it is critical to successful improvement efforts.

By streamlining VADS to focus only on the steps needed to successfully transform the primary and secondary objects, true improvements can be realized. This does not mean downsizing! It does mean doing the right steps in the right order to achieve the value added objective of the VADS. The process of aligning object transformations is akin to a chiropractor aligning the vertebrae of the spine to allow the nervous system to function properly. Often, as in the upcoming insurance company example, it means adding people to a process. The process of aligning object transformations to the value-added objective is the act of tuning a VADS to operate at peak efficiency.

FACTOR # 17   **ALIGNMENT OF VADS OBJECT TRANSFORMATION TO PROCESS FAILURES AND VADS IMPEDIMENTS**

For every action that can go right there is at least one way it can go wrong. There is little likelihood that a flawless process involving people can ever be developed. There are too many variables that cannot be controlled. Chaos Theory teaches that. Part of developing VADS that are as watertight as possible is to take an honest look at where they can breakdown. Once the processes, sequences and object transformations are understood and aligned, it is possible to systematically develop recovery scenarios for when the VADS breaks down.

Breakdowns occur for many reasons. The key is to develop recovery procedures for breakdowns that impact critical objects from properly transforming. This means that each VADS needs to have integrated early warning systems and fail-safe stimulus triggers and procedures. This allows people to identify, avoid or respond to breakdowns as soon as possible.

VADS are tested in two modes. The first test is for basic flow. Here, the impact of volume (how much) and velocity (how fast) is ignored. This tests the VADS in its simplest form as if it were the only thing the organization did. The second test imposes the impact of volume and velocity. Volume represents how many cycles the VADS will be have within a specified time period (hour, day, week, etc.).

Velocity is the speed that VADS cycles will occur. Most seemingly well designed VADS fail because they do not perform well under stress. An illustration from the "I Love Lucy Show" will help make this point.

In one of the most famous "I Love Lucy" episodes, Lucy gets a job in a candy factory. Her job was to simply take chocolates off a conveyor belt and place them in a box. In training, this process was easy enough that even Lucy could do it. What could go wrong? When Lucy started the process, the chocolates were well spaced and the conveyor belt was moving at a manageable rate.

What Lucy had not planned on was the conveyor belt steadily picking up speed (velocity) and the chocolates becoming more tightly spaced (volume). As the volume and velocity increased, Lucy's ability to perform decreased. She started improvising. She placed chocolates in her hat, then her blouse and finally her mouth. Clearly the process had broken down. Lucy's goal turned from getting the chocolates in the box so they could be sold to customers to getting them off the conveyor belt any way she could.

Does this happen in real life? You bet. In one of my consulting assignments in the early 1980's, I consulted to a major insurance company. The claims processing process was not working well. Some claims took only a few days to process, while others took months or never were processed at all. Policy holders were upset to the point of canceling their policies and going to the competition.

This upset the stockholders and that got top management's attention.

The objective of the assignment was to study the claims processing function and recommend corrective action.

When the claims process was first mapped out it appeared to be quite logical and efficient. It wasn't until it was tested under stress (real-life working conditions) that the breakdown was discovered. What happened was this. Claims did not flow evenly throughout the week. There were peaks and valleys to the volume. The company had staffed the function to handle claims as if they came through the organization in a consistent and even volume and velocity. To compound the situation, the company had not factored in the increase new policies had on the expected number of claims it would process.

Claims processing clerks were rated on the number of claims they processed in a day. This metric had been established years ago and never revised. When the volume and velocity picked up, claims processing clerks fell behind. They fell so far behind that they would stuff claims in drawers and cubbyholes to get them off their desks. They lost sight of the goal. The clerks would process just enough claims to meet the benchmark and the rest would be thrown out. In essence, the company set itself up to fail. The clerks acted just like Lucy with the chocolates. This was a classic breakdown on many fronts. These include:

1. The company's management was insensitive to the impact increased business (volume) had on the employees (ignoring one of their stakeholders).

2. The employees were trained to make their numbers rather than to understand how their job added value to customers (processing X number of claims was more important than reimbursing policy holders for their losses).

3. The VADS of processing claims did not properly integrate fail safes into it (claims were not tracked based on each transformation that occurred as they moved through the process).

4. Overworked employees lead to poor morale and resulted in the delay or loss of the claims being processed.

The solution was to:

1. Staff the claims processing function appropriately,

2. Replace the measurement system with a value-added goal around processing claims from receipt through resolution, and

3. Improve the process to incorporate a tracking system that zeroed in on claims that were falling short of the processing goal (i.e. tracking each transformation in terms of it occurring within a certain window of time.)

Volume and velocity play a critical role in understanding where VADS can breakdown. In the implementer's guide, failure analysis and other key factors that contribute to VADS failures are presented in detail.

Chapter Summary

This chapter focused on the factors that build alignment between all the components that go into ensuring that value is delivered to stakeholders as intended. By systematically applying each of the nine alignment factors the changes needed to achieve organizational alignment in how value is added can be identified, explored and acted on. The process can be done top down, bottom up or inside out. It really does not matter where it starts. The key is to know where in the process review is starting so that the proper steps are taken.

When embarking on a quest to align business processes with the strategic objectives of an organization, try not to think of it as a re-engineering or process improvement project. Think of it as an alignment process that will result in the proper level of adjustment. There is no need to label the effort beyond this.

Achieving organizational alignment is the primary goal of HELIX. As VADS become aligned with business objectives and strategic direction, people tend to become more aligned with each other. They understand their role and how they personally add value to others. Value is optimized across all stakeholders and the organization prospers. In the implementer's guide, the nuts and bolts of conducting a HELIX project and the use of related modeling tools are explained in detail.

> **Keep in mind that the goal is to achieve alignment not just to map or document business processes.**

The **HELIX** Factor

The tools are only provided to leverage the effort and are just a means to a greater end.

Questions to reflect on

1. What expectations do your organization's stakeholders have related to the value the organization provides? How does the organization know this?

2. How does your organization's strategic direction support stakeholder needs?

3. Where is your organization going? How will it know when it arrives?

4. What will ensure the long term success of your organization? How do you know that?

5. Who should understand the stakeholder's expectations? Strategic direction? Business strategies?

6. What qualities do good business objectives have?

7. How many of these qualities do your organization's business objectives have?

8. Who should business objectives be written for?

9. At what level do your organization's business objectives align upward (toward stakeholder expectations) and downward (toward VADS and the people that work within them)?

10. What are some of the organizational misalignments that exist?

11. What would your organization be like if people were

focused on adding value rather than defending their
territory?

12. How do work actions correlate with work value?

13. What is a good way to ensure high work quality in
the work being performed?

14. What percentage of your organization's workers, if
asked, could relate their day-to-day actions to how
those actions add value to others?

15. What stimulus triggers are at play in your daily job?
How do you know what actions are needed throughout
the day?

16. What outcomes do not make sense in your
organization? What types of service breakdowns
occur? Why?

17. What Value-added-Delivery Systems do you
participate in?

18. How do your actions transform the objects being
moved through those systems?

19. What process failures occur in your organization? In
the VADS you help support?

FAILURES THAT CAN BE PREDICTED DO
NOT ADD TO THE LEARNING PROCESS

Chapter 6

Executive Overview Managing the Process

What Executives Need to Know to Manage a **HELIX** Project

Chapters 4 and 5 have set the stage for an overview of the HELIX process. This chapter presents a summary of the steps and tools used in a HELIX project. It is intended to provide management with the knowledge needed to monitor a project's progress and to understand how the tools and techniques contribute to the outcome to be achieved. This chapter is also intended to provide a bridge from this text to the case study that is designed for use by those who will actually perform the project.

> **A HELIX project is intended to identify specific changes needed within an organization allowing it to align its work processes with the strategic and business objectives it aspires to achieve.**

HELIX projects can vary in scope. An organization could choose to include all its Value-added Delivery Systems in a project or tighten its focus to only a few. Regardless of the size of the project the process is the same. Below is a checklist and quick reference guide of the key actions that take place in every HELIX project.

Part 1 — Executive Briefing

A. Meet with executive management to review stakeholder needs, strategic direction and supporting objectives

B. Review the business plan

C. Develop clarifying and reflective questions to improve the quality of business plan objectives

D. Identify project objectives and related VADS

E. Confirm team's understanding and build consensus for project scope

F. Present project proposal

Part 2 — Kickoff the Project

A. Identify and select potential team and VADS knowledge worker participants

B. Hold formal kickoff meeting with Team and VADS knowledge workers

C. Confirm that a full and shared understanding of how Stakeholder needs, the strategic direction, business objectives and project objectives exist among all participants.

Part 3 — Perform the Field Work

A. For each VADS included in the project

    1) Conduct First Facilitation Work Session

        a) Review project objectives and goals of work sessions

        b) Facilitate a change analysis (identify

initial improvement opportunities)

c) Facilitate an existing level 1 workflow model

d) Facilitate an existing level 2 workflow model

e) Map the change analysis' current situations to the Level 2 Workflow model

f) Facilitate a proposed level 2 workflow model

g) Map the change analysis' preliminary goals to the proposed level 2 workflow model

2) Conduct First Diagnostic Work Session

a) Formalize the models into usable working papers

b) Test the models for integrity

c) Develop a skeleton for part 2 of the change analysis

d) Test alignments

e) Refine VADS to resolve potential failures

f) Update models and prepare for distribution

g) Develop questions and issues for next facilitation work sessions

3) Conduct Subsequent Facilitation Work Sessions

a) Perform walk-thrus of models

b) Integrate improvement

recommendations

    c)   Obtain consensus

4)   Conduct Subsequent Diagnostic Work Sessions

    a)   Finalize models

    b)   Develop implementation work plans

    c)   Develop implementation cost and resource estimates

    d)   Prepare and package proposal for management

Part 4 — Present Findings to Management

Present the specific findings and recommendations to management on "HOW TO" achieve the improvement objectives of the organization.

PART 1

EXECUTIVE BRIEFING

BUILD AN ALIGNED UNDERSTANDING BETWEEN EXECUTIVE MANAGEMENT AND PROJECT LEADERS

Obtaining executive management's buy-in and approval is critical to any project. In a HELIX project this process is not only critical but a core prerequisite. Therefore, the first step in the HELIX process is to conduct two to three work sessions with management. Each session will last from two to three hours. At those work sessions the team will do the following:

1. Gather Information about the organization's objectives and needs.
2. Formulate a project's objectives and scope.
3. Present a proposal for the project

At the end of the three sessions, management will have a specific proposal that demonstrates a shared understanding of:

1. The improvement objectives to be pursued
2. How those objectives align with the overall business objectives of the organization
3. Which divisions and 3. Which Value-added Delivery Systems will be included in the project
4. Which divisions and departments will be participating in the project
5. How long the project will take to complete

6. What resources will be needed to complete the project

Once the management and the project team agree (aligned) on the work to be completed the project can start.

The total time commitment from each executive management member to complete this effort typically ranges from 6 to 10 hours spread over about 4 to 6 weeks. The actual time needed to complete this portion of the project will depend greatly on the size of the organization and effort to be undertaken. The key to keeping the time short is to conduct this work in a hands-on, face-to-face fashion, with a complete team of the executive management. Keep in mind that this is a collaborative process between the executive management and the project team not a meeting consisting of a set of management directives issued to a team of note takers.

During the first two meetings all participants should expect to share in a productive dialogue resulting in a shared vision of what is to be accomplished and how value will be added to the organization and its stakeholders. Therefore, management needs to select a project team that it respects for its strategic, tactical and critical thinking skills.

With this first step successfully completed, the project can commence on a firm foundation.

PART 2

KICKOFF THE PROJECT

PRESENT A FORMAL ENDORSEMENT OF THE PROJECT AND CREATE INITIAL MOMENTUM

A formal project kickoff demonstrates management's commitment to the project and sets a positive tone for moving forward. Before holding the project kickoff event the full project team and knowledge workers who will participate on the project need to be identified and selected.

The project kickoff should be attended by at least one executive management representative. The division or department heads that will have knowledge workers participating in the project should be present as well. Finally, the project team and knowledge worker participants should be present. If the HELIX project is going to be conducted for an entire company then a modified version of the kickoff should be conducted. Management may want to consider a "Road Show" of multiple kickoff events if the project is geographically dispersed.

The kickoff should contain two parts. The first consists of a briefing of the project's scope and objectives to the attendees. During this segment the management endorses and restates its expectations for the project's outcome. Remember "Factor #5 The Principle of

Context" is important here. The project's objectives must be clear and quantifiable. The team and project participants are introduced. Key time tables are reviewed and final questions addressed.

Part two of the kickoff is social in nature. Typically it consists of a reception with refreshments. The goal of this part of the kickoff is to provide a forum for all project participants and project stakeholders to spend some relaxed time together. If the project is large enough, this could be done at a formal facility. On the other hand, a small project may be kicked off in a conference room. The goal is the same: to present a formal endorsement of the project and to create initial momentum.

PART 3

PERFORM THE FIELD WORK

CONDUCT THE FACILITATION AND DIAGNOSTIC WORK SESSIONS

The field work to be performed in a HELIX project consists of conducting up to 3 facilitation work sessions with the knowledge workers and conducting up to 3 diagnostic work sessions for each VADS included in the study.

FACILITATION WORK SESSIONS

Facilitation work sessions are attended by two HELIX facilitators and the knowledge workers who represent every process group involved in the VADS to be improved. This cross functional and collective knowledge base allows the HELIX facilitators to accelerate the model development process.

Facilitation work sessions are intended to help the session participants identify and quantify the key improvements to VADS needed to support the project's objectives. This is done by interactively developing 4 models with the group over 3 work sessions each lasting about 2.5 hours. The 2.5 hour limit per work session allows knowledge workers to participate in the project without detracting from their ability to perform their normal job function. Each facilitation work session is followed by a diagnostic work session that will be reviewed later.

Each facilitation work session is started by reviewing the objectives of the project, the particular work session and the work completed to date.

In the first facilitation work session the goal is to develop 3 models. During the first few projects, it might take 2 work sessions to complete these three models due to the team's experience levels with HELIX.

The models developed provide a foundation for diagnosing and blueprinting:

1. What changes need to take place to achieve the project improvement objectives (change analysis — current situations)

2. Where in the VADS those changes would need to take place (existing level 1 workflow model)

3. How those changes would improve the VADS (change analysis — preliminary goals)

4. What process groups and systems would be affected by the changes (existing level 1 & 2 workflow models)

5. What the changed VADS would look like (proposed level 2 workflow model)

The three models developed are:

1. Change Analysis

2. Level 1 Workflow Model (Existing)

3. Level 2 Workflow Model (Existing)

4. Level 2 Workflow Model (Proposed)

During subsequent facilitation and diagnostic work sessions the models are refined and tested for their accuracy and completeness.

CHANGE ANALYSIS

The first model to be developed or updated in a work session is the change analysis. The change analysis (CA) is a tabular model that contrasts existing situations (situations needing improvement), with preliminary goals (solutions that constitute an acceptable improvement). The CA is developed interactively with the knowledge worker group, using a flip chart to record the situations and goals. It is very important that the CA model be done first.

The CA sets the stage for achieving the catharsis and revelation **(see Factor # 7 --The Principle of Catharsis and Revelation)** needed to release creativity in the work session. The CA occupies about 45 minutes of the 2.5 hours allocated for the work session.

The change analysis presents two views of a situation that the work session participants believe could be improved. The first view describes the current situation related to a process within a VADS in terms of:

⦿ What is happening,

⦿ Why it happens,

⦿ How much it costs,

- What Makes it undesirable,

- Who is Impacted (loses value) because of it happening

The second view describes a proposed future state of the same VADS process. This future state presents what the work session participants believe would constitute a major improvement to the process. This view describes:

- What should happen,

- When should it happen,

- What would have to change for it to happen,

- Why it is better than the way it is done now,

- How much it will cost or save, and

- Who it will benefit (gain value).

With these two views presented side by side, the contrast between the current way and a new and better way of doing can be easily understood. This contrast provides the first step toward providing the knowledge workers with the rationale and emotional leverage needed to pursue the changes identified. It helps develop the creative tension needed to move the group forward.

Figure 6-1 provides an example of a typical change analysis.

Notice that the statement has defined each adjective in measurable terms. The phrase too long which is vague and a relative term is defined as 45 minutes. Since it is a current situation, it is assumed to be undesirable or bad. The statement also identifies why the current situation is bad and why the preliminary goal is good. Finally, notice that the broad implications of the goal are identified.

In the example, the greatest impact of the change would be the need to change the order processing system.

Remember, the change analysis provides the first point of buy-in to VADS improvements by knowledge workers. By looking at what is bad about the current situation and projecting themselves into what is good about the preliminary goal, the beginning of the creative tension (see Factor # 5 -- The Principle of Context) and leverage needed for change is established.

The facilitator works with the work session participants until 8 to 12 change analysis items have been developed. This is a substantial accomplishment. In the span of about 45 minutes, 8 to 12 specific VADS improvements are identified and defined in measurable terms. Each improvement is based on the consensus of the knowledge workers. The next step is to understand where in the VADS these changes need to occur.

Figure 6-1 -- Change Analysis Example # 2

Change Analysis

Current Situation	Preliminary Goal
1 It takes too long to process sales orders through credit. Too Long = more than 45 minutes from the time the credit manager receives the order from the order desk till the time the order is released to the warehouse for shipping. This is bad because it means that orders received after 2pm cannot be shipped until the next day of business. This results in poor customer service.	The ability to process work orders directly to the warehouse where the customer's available credit line is greater than the order amount and their outstanding balance is current. This would require a change to our order processing system. Specifically, it would require the system to automatically check the order for credit related data and route it to the appropriate location (credit department or warehouse).

LEVEL 1 WORKFLOW MODEL

The next model to be developed in the facilitation work sessions is the level 1 workflow model (WFL1). This model presents a simplified version of the VADS by depicting the process groups and the information they share in order to complete a VADS cycle.

The WFL1 is developed in real time (on a flip chart) at the work session with the knowledge workers. It provides the first complete picture of a VADS on a single piece of paper. It has a very simple and intuitive syntax, making it easy to draw, read and understand. The average WFL1 takes about 15 to 20 minutes to complete during a work session.

MODEL SYNTAX

The WFL1 model has a very limited syntax. This is what allows it to be complete yet simple to understand. Figure 6-2 lists the components of the Level 1 workflow model.

Figure 6-2 – Workflow Level 1 Model (WFL1) Syntax

Symbol	Description
Process Group (oval)	The oval or circle represents a work or process group that participates in the VADS. This group represents a one or more people who performs a specific set of procedures on a VADS. This group can be a sub-organization within the organization (division, department, specific job title or specific work area). The group can also represent outside organizations or people (customers, vendors, government, etc.). An ICON can be substituted for this symbol. However, if ICONS are used they should be consistent through out all models.
File or Data Store (rectangle)	The rectangle represents a file, data store or system. This object can be a file cabinet, ledger card, a computer system or any other non-human repository for storing information. An ICON can be substituted for this symbol. However, if ICONS are used they should be consistent through out all models

Figure 6-2 - – Workflow Level 1 Model (WFL1) syntax (cont.)

Symbol	Description
Scope Constraint Boundary	The arc represents a constraint or boundary. It denotes an intentional limitation in the scope of the model. The text behind the arc is used to clarify the scope limitation. For instance, in a sales VADS, the model may not reflect how the customer decided to place an order. If this information was not going to be reflected in the VADS, a scope constraint boundary would be placed on the edge of the customer process group to reflect the scope limitation.
To WFL1 - 1.4 To WFL1 - 2.1 **Inbound / Outbound "T"s.**	The "T" represents a link between two models. This linkage can be inbound (feeding this model) or outbound (feeding another model.) The direction of the connection is indicated by the arrow. Arrows pointing toward the top of the "T" are outbound. Arrows pointing away from the "T" are inbound. The text at the end of the "T" is the reference to the model being referenced. For every "T" inbound or outbound, there is a corresponding outbound or inbound "T" in the referenced model..

Figure 6-2 - – Workflow Level 1 Model (WFL1) syntax (cont.)

Symbol	Description
⑤ Text of what is being transferred	The arrow and associated numbered text represents the transfer of data between two process groups or a process group and a data store. The arrow points in the direction of the information movement. A two-headed arrow represents an interaction such as a conversation or interface with a system. The number represents the sequence in which the communication takes place in context to the entire model. When the transfer is between two process groups, or from a system to a process group, it represents both information and stimulus trigger (an indication that action is needed).
③ Interaction or Conversation	

To draw the model, the facilitator simply has the knowledge workers talk their way through the VADS. As the process gets described, the facilitator records the steps using the level 1 workflow model format. In this way, the participants do not need to understand how to construct a model. They merely need to understand how the VADS in question is performed.

Since a representative from every work area contributing to the VADS is present, the model can be completed very quickly (10 to 15 minutes). The model also identifies missing knowledge workers. For each process group identified on the model, there should be a corresponding knowledge worker present at the work session. The only exception to this rule is when the process group identified is a process groups that is not part of the organization (customers, vendors, government, etc.).

The completed model presents the process groups involved in the VADS and what is communicated between them in order to successfully complete a single VADS cycle (see figure 6-3).

Notice in figure 6-3 how each line of communication between the process groups is numbered. This number indicates the sequence of events that takes place to move, in this case, a customer's desire for product through the point where the order is paid for and payment is posted. What the model does not reflect are the internal steps each process group takes to move information to the next process group. This will be done in the next model to be developed. When a condition arises that would require the VADS to branch in two or more directions, thus breaking the sequence of events, the facilitator requests that the group develop an assumption list.

The assumption list appears at the top of the model. In the above example the assumption is:

SALES ORDERS ON ACCOUNT WHEN THE CUSTOMER'S CREDIT LIMIT IS GOOD, INVENTORY IS AVAILABLE AND THE CUSTOMER PAYS ON TIME

When an assumption occurs it implies that there are other possible ways the VADS cycle can be performed. For example: If sales orders can be "on account," there is an implied assumption that a sales order can be processed for customers who do not have accounts. Similarly, if a customer's credit limit can be good, then there must be instances when the customer's credit limit is bad. Based on the above assumption statement, as many as 16 variations could exist for selling product. If some of those 16 variations are part of the way the company wants to do business then they should be considered for inclusion and modeled. For those variations that represent anomalies in the normal VADS cycle no new WFL1 models need to be done. These deviations from the norm will be handled during the failure analysis stage of the diagnostic work session.

When the WFL1 model is complete the project team and knowledge workers have a complete picture of the way a VADS currently functions. This will be critical to building the level 2 workflow model and in correlating where change analysis items occur along the process flow.

Figure 6-3 — Level 1 Workflow (WFL1) Model

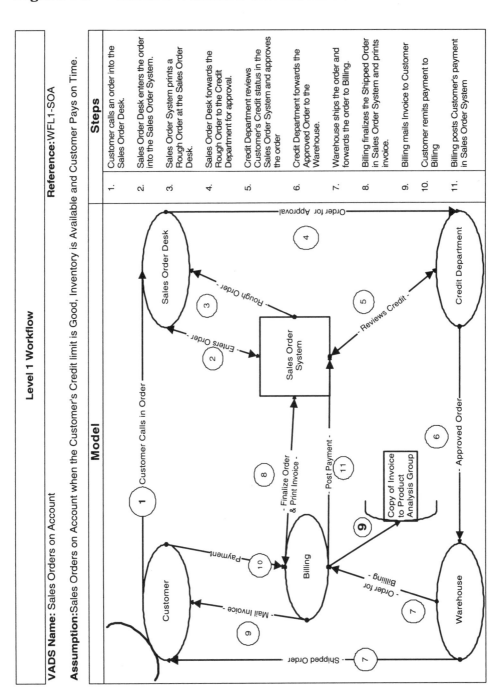

Level 1 Workflow

VADS Name: Sales Orders on Account

Reference: WFL1-SOA

Assumption: Sales Orders on Account when the Customer's Credit limit is Good, Inventory is Available and Customer Pays on Time.

Steps

1. Customer calls an order into the Sales Order Desk.

2. Sales Order Desk enters the order into the Sales Order System.

3. Sales Order System prints a Rough Order at the Sales Order Desk.

4. Sales Order Desk forwards the Rough Order to the Credit Department for approval.

5. Credit Department reviews Customer's Credit status in the Sales Order System and approves the order

6. Credit Department forwards the Approved Order to the Warehouse.

7. Warehouse ships the order and forwards the order to Billing.

8. Billing finalizes the Shipped Order in Sales Order System and prints invoice.

9. Billing mails Invoice to Customer

10. Customer remits payment to Billing

11. Billing posts Customer's payment in Sales Order System

Model

LEVEL 2 WORKFLOW MODEL

After about an hour into the 2 1/2 hour facilitation work session, the group has defined two models: 1) a change analysis that identifies 8 to 12 VADS improvements and 2) a level 1 workflow model that presents the current way the VADS moves information from one process group to another. The next step is to define the procedures that each process group takes to transform the information being moved between process groups to complete a VADS cycle. The level 2 workflow (WFL2) model accomplishes this and is the next model to be developed in the work session.

The WFL2 expands the WFL1 model to show the phases and procedures needed to move a VADS cycle from its beginning point through its completion. The model is tabular in form (rows and columns). Each column on the model represents a phase of the VADS cycle. The phases are sequentially dependent on each other. Phase B cannot be done until Phase A is completed. Phase C cannot be done until Phase B is completed and so on.

To build the model, the facilitator works interactively with the knowledge workers to recast and expand the WFL1 model into the WFL2 format **(see Figure 6-4)** .

Each phase (column) of the WFL2 model is comprised of 5 components.

1. **Beginning Status** - The beginning status appears at the top of each column of the model. It indicates the status of the primary object before the subsequent procedures take place.

2. **Procedures** - The procedures appear beneath the beginning status. The procedures list the actions that must take place to move the object to the ending status. These procedures reflect all the information communication steps found in the WFL1 model, plus the critical actions taken within each of the process groups.

3. **Ending Status** - The ending status appears next on the model. It reflects the status of the primary object of the VADS after the procedures have taken place. The ending status becomes the beginning status of the next phase on the model.

4. **Lapsed Time** - The lapsed time is the time it takes to complete the related phase of the VADS. It can be expressed in any unit of time (days, hours, minutes, etc.). Comparing lapsed time with level of effort can help to identify workflow bottlenecks and improvement opportunities. If the lapsed time is greater than the level of effort, then there are delays that could present an opportunity for improvement.

5. **Level of Effort** - The level of effort represents the actual labor needed to perform the procedures of the VADS phase. This can also be expressed in any unit of time. The cost per hour of those performing the VADS, times the total hours of effort provides an estimate of the cost to complete one cycle of the VADS.

Figure 6-4 – Workflow Level 2 (WFL2) Model

	Phase A	Phase B	Phase C
Beg. Status	A customer wanting to order product	Rough sales order pending credit approval	Approved sales order ready for shipping
P R O C E D U R E S	1 The customer calls the order desk with an order. 2 Order desk identifies customer and enters order via order entry screen. 3 Inventory availability and ship dates are verified with customer. 4 Rough order is printed and sent to credit for approval.	1 Credit receives rough order from the order desk. 2 Credit retrieves order from system and verifies the credit limit. 3 Credit reviews customer's outstanding A/R. 4 Credit approves order on system, stamps it approved and forwards it to warehouse for shipping.	1 Warehouse receives order from credit. 2 Warehouse picks order and updates quantities picked on the order form. 3 Warehouse packages and ships order to customer 4 Warehouse sends shipped order to Billing.
End Status	Rough sales order pending credit approval	Approved sales order ready for shipping	Shipped sales order ready for billing
Elapsed Time	5 minutes	2 days	1 day
Effort	5 minutes	45 minutes	1 hour

Figure 6-4 – Workflow Level 2 (WFL2) Model (cont.)

	Phase E	Phase D
Beg. Status	Billed sales order pending collection	Shipped sales order ready for billing
P R O C E D U R E S	1 Customer receives the invoice. 2 Customer sends payment to billing. 3 Billing retrieves the customer's invoice from the system and posts the payment. 4 The system updates the customer's credit limit and accounts receivable balance.	1 Billing receives order from warehouse. 2 Billing retrieves order from the system and enters the actual quantities shipped. 3 The system updates inventory, adjusts the customer credit limit and creates the invoice. 4 Billing prints the invoice and mails to customer.
End Status	Collected sales order	Billed sales order pending collection
Lapsed Time	45 days	2 hours
Effort	10 minutes	10 minutes

The WFL2 model provides a snapshot of the phases, procedures, time frames and effort needed to complete a single cycle of a VADS. Once the number of cycles that occur per year are established, an estimate of the total cost of the VADS to the company can be developed. This can then be evaluated to determine the VADS contribution to the organization and to establish its ROI or cost benefit. A simplified example illustrates this set of calculations:

Assumption:

1. The average cost of an employee is $26 per hour.

2. The total level of effort to complete the sales order VADS process is 4 hours and 35 minutes.

3. The total number of VADS cycles completed each year equals 6,000.

The total cost of a VADS cycle is calculated as follows: $26 per hour times 4 hours and 35 minutes equals $119.16

The total annual cost of the VADS is 6,000 cycles times $119.16 or $714,960.

In real projects the team would use average costs per phase of the VADS to compute cycle and annual costs of labor to compute annual VADS costs. Also, the level of effort would include factors for errors that happen from time-to-time in the VADS. These factors would be determined during the mapping of the change analysis to the WFL2 and during failure analysis.

The WFL2 also provides insights as to the number of objects being transformed (changed) during each cycle of the VADS. With that knowledge the group can assess whether the record-keeping and information systems are being properly updated to reflect these transformations.

> **The WFL2 model becomes a focal point for linking situations identified in the change analysis to specific phases and procedures within the VADS.**

> **It becomes the vehicle for conceptualizing and visualizing the changes needed to achieve the project improvement objectives and goals identified in the change analysis.**

The level 2 workflow model is the pivotal model of a HELIX discovery project. Around this model a framework can be established for:

1. Understanding where specific improvement opportunities exist within the context of how work is done.

2. Pinpointing flaws and improvement opportunities in existing information systems and work procedures that support VADS.

3. Establishing the cost / benefit relationship of the VADS to the organization and its stakeholders.

4. Aligning business objectives of the organization to the physical work actions that achieve those objectives.

5. Conceptualizing new VADS and related systems, policies and procedures to achieve improvements.

With the WFL2 model in place, the facilitator can now work with the group to verify that the current situations identified about an hour or so earlier actually occur in the VADS being modeled. This is done by mapping the current situations into the WFL2 model.

MAPPING THE CHANGE ANALYSIS CURRENT SITUATIONS TO THE   LEVEL 2 WORKFLOW MODEL

HELIX has built in proofs of correctness. The first proof of correctness is to correlate (map) the current situations identified in the change analysis to the VADS level 2 workflow model. Again, this is done interactively with the knowledge workers. The process consists of the facilitator selecting the first situation from the change analysis (S1) and asking the work session participants to identify where the situation occurs on the model. Once identified, the facilitator posts the situation number on the model next to the phase or procedure being reviewed. The same process is done for identifying where the project's objectives are being hampered. This is indicated by placing the project objective number (PO#) affected next to the phase or procedure being reviewed.

The clustering of the existing situations on the WFL2 draws the eye to specific areas of the model. Reviewing these clusters provides clues as to where change will most likely be needed to streamline the VADS, correct inherent flaws and achieve the preliminary goals and related project objectives. When situation clusters are accompanied by large differences between the lapsed time and level of effort data for a phase, bottlenecks in workflows are most likely to exist. Figure 6-5 represents a completed WFL2 model.

Figure 6-5 — WFL2 Model after Mapping of Current Situations

	Phase A	Phase B	Phase C
Beg. Status	A customer wanting to order product [PO1]	Rough sales order pending credit approval [S1] [PO1]	Approved sales order ready for shipping [PO1]
P R O C E D U R E S	1 The customer calls the order desk with an order. 2 Order desk identifies customer and enters order via order entry screen. [S2] [PO2] [PO4] 3 Inventory availability and ship dates are verified with customer. 4 Rough order is printed and sent to credit for approval.	1 Credit receives rough order from the order desk. 2 Credit retrieves order from system and verifies the credit limit. 3 Credit reviews customer's outstanding A/R. [S3] 4 Credit approves order on system, stamps it approved and forwards it to warehouse for shipping.	1 Warehouse receives order from credit. 2 Warehouse picks order and updates quantities picked on the order form. [S2] 3 Warehouse packages and ships order to customer. 4 Warehouse sends shipped order to Billing.
End Status	Rough sales order pending credit approval	Approved sales order ready for shipping	Shipped sales order ready for billing
Lapsed Time	5 minutes	2 days	1 day
Effort	5 minutes	45 minutes	1 hour

Figure 6-5 — WFL2 Model after Mapping of Current Situations (cont.)

	Phase D	Phase E
Beg. Status	Shipped sales order ready for billing	Billed sales order pending collection
PROCEDURES	1 Billing receives order from warehouse. 2 Billing retrieves order from the system and enters the actual quantities shipped. 3 The system updates inventory, adjusts the customer credit limit and creates the invoice. 4 Billing prints the invoice and mails to customer.	1 Customer receives the invoice. 2 Customer sends payment to billing. **S3** 3 Billing retrieves the customer's invoice from the system and posts the payment. 4 The system updates the customer's credit limit and accounts receivable balance.
End Status	Billed sales order pending collection	Collected sales order
Lapsed Time	2 hours	45 days
Effort	10 minutes	10 minutes

This correlation process is the first step in helping the VADS' knowledge workers visualize change. It helps them pinpoint where improvements need to be made within the VADS's.

> **Probably for the first time they will have a "Big-Picture" understanding of how their work relates to other coworkers and customers (Factor # 11 -- Alignment of Business Objectives to VADS and process groups)**

This is very significant. At this point the group is ready to create a new WFL2 that will depict the VADS as it could be.

Figure 6-6 summarizes what has been accomplished so far in the first facilitation work session.

Figure 6-6 — Summary of Mapping Current Situations to Existing WFL2

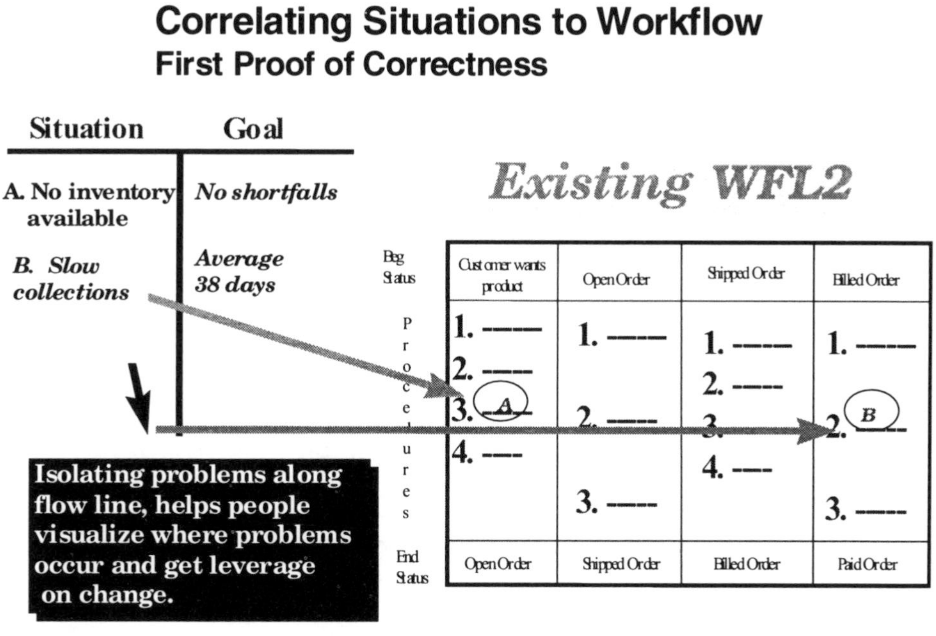

Correlating Situations to Workflow
First Proof of Correctness

The next step is to develop a new WFL2 model that incorporates the achievement of the project objectives and preliminary goals.

BUILDING A PROPOSED LEVEL 2 WORKFLOW MODEL WITH CORRELATED PROJECT OBJECTIVES AND PRELIMINARY GOALS

The final step of the first facilitation work session is to transition from how a VADS works today to a vision of how it could work in the future. This future state for the VADS takes the form of a proposed level 2 workflow (PWFL2). The original WFL2 depicted the way work is performed today and how the current situations related to it. Likewise, the PWFL2 depicts how work could be performed in the future and where the project objectives and preliminary goals are achieved within it.

By the end of the work session, the group will have produced a proposed VADS that they collectively can support and promote to their coworkers. They will be able to articulate how the changes being proposed achieve their improvement goals as well as those of the organization. After just 2 1/2 hours a significant step toward aligning business objectives to workflows will have been achieved (Factor 11 -- Alignment of Business Objectives to Value-added Delivery Systems).

The areas on the model that have been changed are highlighted. Additionally, each project objective (PO) and each preliminary goal (PG) that relate to the workflow is posted on to the model next to where they are achieved. This highlighting and posting process makes it very easy to understand where change will take place and what the benefits of those changes will be **(see Figure 6-7)**.

Figure 6-7 — Example of a Proposed WFL2 Model

	Phase A	Phase B	Phase C	Phase D
Beg. Status	A customer wanting to order product	Approved sales order ready for shipping	Shipped sales order ready for billing	Billed sales order pending collection
PROCEDURES	1 The customer calls the order desk with an order. **Order Entry Process** 2 **Order desk identifies the customer and verifies that their outstanding balance is current via the order entry screen. The system flags the order as clearing O/S Balance review.** [PG1] 3 **For each item ordered, the order desk verifies the inventory is available and confirms ship dates.** [PG2] [PO2] [PO4] 4 **Upon completion of the order, the system reserves the inventory being ordered, sets its status to "Approved" and prints it directly to the warehouse printer.** [PG1] [PG3]	1 Warehouse receives order via printer. 2 Warehouse picks order and updates quantities picked on the order form. 3 Warehouse packages and ships order to customer. 4 Warehouse sends shipped order to billing.	1 Billing receives order from warehouse. 2 Billing retrieves order from the system and enters the actual quantities shipped. 3 The system updates inventory, adjusts the customer credit limit and creates the invoice. 4 Billing prints the invoice and mails to customer.	1 Customer receives the invoice. 2 Customer sends payment to billing. 3 Billing retrieves the customer's invoice from the system and posts the payment. 4 The system updates the customer's credit limit and accounts receivable balance.
End Status	Approved sales order ready for shipping	Shipped sales order ready for billing [PO1]	Billed sales order pending collection	Collected sales order
Lapsed Time	5 minutes [PO1]	1 day [PO1]	2 hours	45 days
Effort	5 minutes	1 hour	10 minutes	10 minutes

139

Figure 6-8 illustrates the process of mapping preliminary goals to the proposed WFL2.

Once the proposed WFL2 has been completed, the first facilitation work session is complete. Within 2.5 hours of collective and collaborative effort the group has produced a:

1. Change analysis

   8 to 12 improvement concepts that directly relate to a VADS

2. Level 1 workflow model

   Depicts who is involved in the VADS and what is communicated between process groups

3. Existing level 2 workflow model

   Expands the WFL1 by adding work procedures and then correlates current situations from the change analysis to verify that the issues being discussed are relevant to the VADS being explored.

4. Proposed level 2 workflow model

   A conceptual view of how the VADS might be changed to achieve related project objectives and the preliminary goals identified in the change analysis.

The next step in the process is for the project team to perform a series of diagnostics on the data collected.

Figure 6-8 — Summary of Mapping Preliminary Goals to the Proposed WFL2

Correlating Goals to Conceptual Workflow Second Proof of Correctness

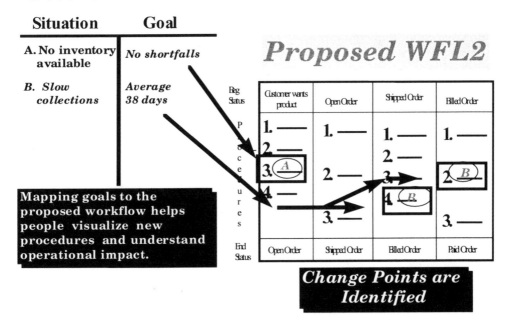

DIAGNOSTIC WORK SESSIONS

After each facilitation work session the core project team uses the models and other information developed and conducts a post-diagnostic work session. Each diagnostic work session should be done within 24 hours of the facilitation work session. Doing the diagnostics as close to the facilitation as possible minimizes the possibility of misinterpretations of the models and notes that were collected. The goal of the diagnostic work session is to:

1. Test the models developed

2. Ensure that the proposed VADS are aligned with the project objectives

3. Estimate the time and cost to implement improvements and

4. Prepare for subsequent facilitation work sessions or presentations.

Since there are only three facilitation work sessions, there are only three diagnostic work sessions for any one VADS.

DIAGNOSTIC WORK SESSION # 1

The first diagnostic work session consists of seven major activities:

1. Formalize the models into usable working papers

2. Test the models for integrity

3. Develop skeleton of part 2 of the change analysis

4. Test alignments

5. Refine VADS for potential failures

6. Update models and prepare for distribution

7. Develop questions and issues for the next facilitation work session.

At the beginning of the first diagnostic work session, the team has its knowledge of the facilitation session plus the data it collected on the flip charts. The flip chart data consists of:

1. Change analysis (CA) — Where opportunities for improvement exist (current situations) and what those improvements might look like (preliminary goals).

2. Existing level 1 workflow (WFL1) — The process groups, information and communications needed to complete a VADS cycle.

3. Existing level 2 workflow (EWFL2) — The existing phases, procedures and object transformations needed to complete a VADS cycle.

4. Current situations correlated to the WFL1 - First proof of correctness that verifies the opportunities for improvement related to the VADS being reviewed.

5. Proposed level 2 workflow (PWFL2) — The proposed phases, procedures and object transformations needed to complete a VADS cycle.

6. Preliminary goals correlated to the WFL2 - Second proof of correctness that verifies the project objectives and proposed improvements are achieved through the proposed VADS.

The challenge facing the team is to get the data off the flip charts and out of their heads and into usable working papers so the data can be reviewed and tested. Diagnostic work sessions two and three will be presented later in this section.

Summarizing the Diagnostic Work Session and Knowledge Gained

The data in the team's head needs to be written up on two working papers. The first is a work session summary. The work session summary provides:

1. A brief description of the work session's goals

2. The names of those in attendance

3. A brief description of the discussions that took place

4. The team's observations about the session

5. The action items agreed to

6. The date and time of the next work session.

This summary should be only a page or two in length.

The next working paper is a Knowledge Summary. The knowledge summary contains any key information the team believes is important that is not represented on the flip charts. Think of it as a running journal that records the team's understanding of the organization's needs in the context of the project. The goal is to keep the team consciously aware of its knowledge gains throughout the process. This short documentation process helps reinforce those gains.

FORMALIZING THE MODELS

The next step in the diagnostic process is to transcribe the flip chart version of the model generated in the facilitation work session on to 8.5 x 11 or 11 x 17 inch paper. This process can be done manually or with the aid of a computer (preferred). During this transcription the team tests and updates the models for their integrity and completeness. This is done by applying a set of associated rules to each model.

For example the change analysis statements are each tested for their compliance to the following rules:

For each situation, the team should verify that it clearly states:

1. What is happening

2. Why it happens

3. How much it costs

4. What makes it undesirable and

5. Who is impacted (loses value) because of it happening?

Where the situation falls short in answering these questions, the team should prepare questions for the next work session. If the questions will require some research to answer, the team provides the knowledge workers with the questions before the next work session.

The same process is done for each preliminary goal. Each goal should be tested to ensure that it clearly states:

1   What should happen

2   When it should happen

3   What would have to change for it to happen

4   Why it is better than the way it is done now

5   How much it will save and

6   Who will benefit (gain value) from the improvement.

Where the preliminary goals do not pass this diagnostic test, the team should formulate and provide questions for the knowledge workers to research and answer.

As a result of the diagnostics performed on the first change analysis item presented earlier, the team may have expanded the item to be more definitive.

Figure 6-9 depicts the CA that has been expanded to provide more substance and cost benefit data. The expanded CA statements conform to all the rules required to make a complete change analysis. The expansion of the CA was accomplished by the team asking the knowledge worker representatives to clarify questions about the current situation and preliminary goal. This clarification process could have taken place during the diagnostic work sessions or in a subsequent facilitation work session.

The team would perform similar diagnostics on each of the models developed. Each model has rules that need to be applied. The result is a very meaningful set of models that can be shared with the knowledge workers and fine-tuned as needed to achieve buy-in.

Figure 6-9 – Example of an Expanded Change Analysis Item

#	Current Situation	E WFL2	Preliminary Goal	P WFL2
1	It takes too long to process sales orders through Credit. Too Long = more than 45 minutes from the time the Credit Manager receives the order from the order desk until the time the order is released to the warehouse for shipping. This is bad because it means that orders received after 2p.m. cannot be shipped until the next day of business. This results in poor customer service. This occurs due to the volume of orders (greater than 150 a day) coupled with the number of steps that are taken to review and approve credit and complete the order. Based on an average wage of $30 an hour and 45 minute of processing time, the cost to approve a sales order is $22.50. Given a volume of 150 orders a day, it requires about 14 Credit staff to keep up with the volume. The average daily cost to process orders through Credit is about $3,375 a day.		The ability to send work orders directly to the warehouse where the customer's available credit line is greater than the order amount and their outstanding balance is current. This would require a change to the order processing system to support the automatic credit checking process and related electronic transmission of orders to the warehouse and Credit Department. Immediately upon the order desk completing the entry of the order, the system would credit check the order and electronically route it directly to the warehouse (approved) or the Credit Department (denied) for the appropriate action. Testing and routing of an order should take under one minute. This is good because it reduces the overall order processing time by at least 44 minutes for orders that pass the automatic credit check. This directly supports the project objective: to ship orders within 24 hours of receipt.	

Figure 6-9 – Example of an Expanded Change Analysis Item (cont.)

#	Current Situation	E WFL2	Preliminary Goal	P WFL2
1	Given the objective to ship orders within 24 hours of receipt, reducing the time required to process orders through Credit supports this objective and improves customer service levels. Reducing the time it takes to approve orders will also reduce the cost of order processing thereby providing value to the owners.		It is estimated that approximately 91% (137 per day) of the orders received would clear this credit checking process. Based on the current cost of $22.50 to credit check an order, this improvement would result in five year savings of over $3 million ($740k X 5 - $600k) or $600 thousand annually. Based on a limited review, the cost to modify the order processing system and to implement the new process is estimated between $180,000 and $600,000. The expected return on investment in the first year should range from 23% to 77% depending on the actual implementation costs The above savings would benefit the company by providing a net saving of about $140,000 the first year and $740,000 in subsequent years. Customers would benefit from this change in that they would receive their shipments up to 24 hours sooner. With the reduced number of orders flowing to the Credit Department, the department can focus its full attention on problem orders and avoid adding new staff in the future.	

Two new models are developed during the diagnostic work session. The first is an expansion of the change analysis (CA2). This model identifies:

1. The risk variables and uncontrollable aspects of those variables associated with each preliminary goal.

2. Any limitations and constraints imposed by the organization for achieving the goals and objectives.

3. Realistic and achievable goals that factor in the two items above.

The second model is a failure analysis (FA). This analysis examines each procedure in the proposed WFL2 and determines the impact of potential failures in the process. The result is the introduction of sufficient controls and monitoring procedures to cost-effectively ensure that any failures occurring during a VADS cycle are minimized and corrected quickly. The FA process allows the team to work from a primary version of a VADS and resolve any process anomalies that might occur during the workflow process.

For example, one of the assumptions in the WFL1 developed above is that the customer's credit limit is sufficient to cover the value of the order being placed. During failure analysis this assumption would be challenged and procedures developed for when the customer's credit limit is insufficient. Likewise, each procedure on the WFL2 model would be challenged.

What happens if procedure C4 (Billing prints the invoice and mails to customer) on the PWFL2 does not take place? What is the impact on the collection phase of the VADS? When will the company know this has the order was never billed to the customer? What procedures can be set in place to either prevent this from happening or detect its happening as close to the invoices being mailed as possible?

These types of diagnostics and questions help the team develop VADS that are functional and efficient.

> **Through failure analysis needless controls are designed out of the VADS, while essential functional controls that protect stakeholder interests are designed into the VADS.**

The final step in the first diagnostic work session is to complete a series of alignment matrices. These matrices provide a clear correlation between the proposed improvements and the alignment chain presented earlier in this text.

The first alignment worksheet takes the form of a VADS Summary. This summary aligns

1. Stakeholder needs to strategic direction

2. Strategic direction to business objectives

3. Business objectives to value-added delivery systems and process groups.

It also presents a context for what the VADS is and why it is important to the organization.

The second alignment worksheet is a Level 1 Workflow Summary. This summary presents the alignment between:

1. Process groups to information being shared and moved, and

2. Stimulus triggers to process group actions.

This ensures that the proposed changes and VADS are understood at a cause and effect level. It tests the practicality of the workflow at a very detailed level.

The final alignment worksheet is a Level 2 workflow summary. This summary presents the alignment between:

1. Sequence of processes to actions taken

2. Process failures to VADS impediment

3. Information movement to object transformation

4. Object transformation to value-added.

This worksheet links key components of the workflow to ensure that it is as efficient and accurate as possible.

The implementer's guide and case study provides an in-depth explanation of all the diagnostic steps to be performed and examples of the models completed.

By the end of the first diagnostic work session, the major work to develop a model of what changes need to take place to achieve the project objectives and proposed goals has been completed. The remaining facilitation work sessions and subsequent diagnostic work sessions primarily serve to fine-tune the models and to develop the work plans needed to implement the changes defined.

CONDUCT SUBSEQUENT FACILITATION WORK SESSIONS

During the second and third facilitation work sessions the models are reviewed with the knowledge workers. Further improvements are integrated into the models, and consensus and closure are achieved.

By the end of the third facilitation work session the project team and the participating knowledge workers share a single vision of the future for:

1. How The VADS will be changed.

2. How those changes align with the organization's business objectives.

3. How those changes will increase the value being added to stakeholders.

Each knowledge worker will have a clear understanding of how their work efforts contribute to the broader needs of the organization. These knowledge workers will serve as implementation leaders as the project moves to its next phase.

CONDUCT SUBSEQUENT DIAGNOSTIC WORK SESSIONS

During the second and third diagnostic work session the project team:

1. Finalizes the models

2. Develops implementation work plans

3. Develops implementation costs and resource estimates

4. Prepares an implementation proposal for management.

Finally, the team and key knowledge workers present the recommendations to management with the goal of receiving approval to begin implementation.

> **Typically, the ROI on the proposed improvements are so large (500% to 1,000%) that the presentation is merely a formality and approval is virtually always granted.**

FOR BEST RESULTS, MAKE YOUR POINT
CLEAR AND EASY TO UNDERSTAND.

PART 4   PRESENT THE FINDINGS TO MANAGEMENT

Once all the field work is complete, the team needs to package its findings and present them to management. The presentation should be kept to under one hour. Thirty minutes would be a preferable time-frame to make the presentation. The presentation should begin with a review of the project objectives and move directly into the findings and recommendations. The findings should be focused on their value-added attributes and not on the process. For example, one finding might be:

An increase in revenue of $300,000 a year can be achieved by changing the way we process orders.

This finding focuses on results not on how to achieve them. Each finding should be followed by a recommendation. It might read something like this:

To realize this $300,000 improvement we recommend that management approve a project to streamline the order processing workflow and related systems. The cost to do this will be ....

At the end of the presentation a summary of findings and recommendations should be presented in handout form. The summary should consist of a four column table. The first column should present findings (the payback). The second column should present recommendations. The third column should present costs to implement and related pay back.   The fourth column should present the time needed to complete the recommended action and the time needed to achieve the payback.

This approach will keep the findings presentation short and provide compelling reasons to proceed. If the company has a minimum ROI requirement for projects then that too should be presented. The presentation, assuming dramatic improvements can be achieved, should be simply a formality.   Historically, recommendations from **HELIX** based projects are quickly approved.

CHAPTER SUMMARY

This chapter provided an overview of the tools and techniques deployed during a HELIX project. This high-level overview was designed to provide sufficient knowledge of the HELIX process without getting bogged down in too much detail. "The *HELIX Factor II -- The Implementer's Guide and Case Study Workbook*" provides a manual on how to conduct a HELIX projects. It is recommended for the actual project team's use.

At this point, you should have a basic understanding of:

1. The key models produced

2. The goals of each work session

3. A sense of how HELIX provides the consensus, shared vision and practical improvements needed to achieve greater alignment and value between the organization and its stakeholders,

This chapter also serves as a quick reference for managers overseeing a HELIX project. It provides the highlights needed to track a project's progress.

Figure 6-10 is a summary of all the key steps completed in a HELIX project.

Figure 6-10 — Summary of HELIX

Summary of the HELIX Method

	Phase A	Phase B	Phase C
Beg. Status	Executive Briefing	Project Ready for Kick-off	Project Ready for 1st Facilitation Work Session
P R O C E D U R E S	1 Review Stakeholder Needs, Strategic Direction & Supporting Objectives 2 Review Business Plan 3 Develop Questions for Executives 4 Confirm Team's Understanding & Build Consensus for Project Scope 5 Present Project Proposal	1 Identify Potential Team & VADS Knowledge Worker Participants 2 Select Project Team & VADS Knowledge Workers 3 Hold Kick-off Meeting With Team & VADS Knowledge Workers 4 Confirm Team's and Knowledge Worker's Full Understanding of the Correlation Between Stakeholder Needs, Strategic Direction and Project Goals	1 Review Project Objectives & Goal of Work Session 2 Facilitate a Change Analysis - CA (8 to 12 items) 3 Facilitate an Existing Level 1 Workflow (WFL1) 4 Facilitate an Existing Level 2 Workflow (EWFL2) 5 Map the CA Current Situations to EWFL2 6 Facilitate a Proposed Level 2 Workflow (PWFL2) 7 MAP Project Goals and CA Preliminary Goals to PWFL2
End Status	Project Ready for Kick-off	Project Ready for 1st Facilitation Work Session	Project Ready for 1st Diagnostic Work Session
Effort	10 Hours Per Project	4 Hours Per Project	2.5 Hours Per VADS Per Participant (25 to 45 hours)

Figure 6-10 — Summary of HELIX (cont.)

Summary of the HELIX Method

	Phase D	Phase E	Phase F
Beg. Status	Project Ready for 1st Diagnostic Work Session	Project Ready for Subsequent Facilitation Work Sessions	Project Ready for Subsequent Diagnostic Work Sessions
P R O C E D U R E S	1 Summarize Knowledge Gained 2 Formalize CA, WFL1, EWFL2, PWFL2 3 Conduct Diagnostic Tests on CA, WFL1, EWFL2, PWFL2 4 Complete Alignment Diagnostic Worksheets 5 Conduct a Failure Analysis & Refine PWFL2 6 Prepare Follow-up Questions for Next Facilitation Work Session	1 Review Models, Diagnostic Issues and Questions With Knowledge Workers 2 Update Models Based on Clarifications & Insights Received From Knowledge Workers 3 Conduct Final Walk Throughs 4 Obtain Consensus on the CA Preliminary Goals and the PWFL2 5 Outline Action Steps for Implementation	1 Finalize Improvement Recommendations 2 Finalize & Organize Working Papers 3 Develop VADS Level Implementation Plan 4 Develop VADS Level Implementation Cost Estimates 5 Present Findings to Management
End Status	Project Ready for Subsequent Facilitation Work Sessions	Project Ready for Subsequent Diagnostic Work Sessions	Project ready for Implementation
Effort	8 Hours Per VADS Per Project Team Member (16 hours)	5 Hours Per VADS Per Participant (50 to 90 hours)	16 Hours Per VADS (48 hours)

QUESTIONS TO REFLECT ON

1. What makes the executive briefing and project kickoff a critical part of a HELIX project?
2. Why do the knowledge worker participants need to represent the cross-functional nature of the VADS being reviewed?
3. What skill sets must a work session facilitator have?
4. Why is so much emphasis placed on developing clear and measurable current situations and preliminary goals?
5. How are consensus and buy-in achieved among the knowledge workers throughout the project?
6. What value does the output of the project provide the organization?
7. How long would a typical project take assuming it was limited to reviewing 3 VADS'?
8. What makes the proposed level 2 workflow so important?
9. What areas of YOUR organization might benefit from a HELIX project?

CLOSING COMMENTS

You have completed The HELIX Factor. Thank you for taking your valuable time to explore the time tested philosophies, concepts and tools needed to successfully discover how to improve and align an organization with its business processes. I sincerely hope you have found your time well spent. It is only through the value you and others receive from this book that my time in writing it is justified. Below is a quick wrap up of some key points to remember.

Factors 1 through 8 provide a foundation for approaching projects with the correct mind-set. The need to focus on VADS, discovery, collaboration and context are critical to remember. Ways to approach objectives and build momentum is key to achieving meaningful results.

Factors 9 through 17 provide a vision of how to achieve alignment from the expectations of the stakeholders (customers, employees, owners, vendors and community) to the actual work steps that take place to deliver value. Remember, that without alignment virtually any success achieved is often coincidental to effort. From the top to the bottom, from inside out and outside in the people doing the work and receiving the value must share the same expectations.

The executive overview of the HELIX process provides the essential knowledge needed to understand the tools and techniques used in and to monitor the progress of a HELIX project.

If this approach makes sense to you, then it is time to take action and develop a team that can take on its first HELIX project. This requires each team member to read **"The HELIX Factor"** and to work through the **"The HELIX Factor II"** the implementer's guide. The guide presents step-by-step instructions on how to conduct a HELIX project from identifying and organizing a project, conducting facilitation and post diagnostic work sessions, to presenting findings to management. The implementer's guide serves as a "HOW TO" and an ongoing reference guide and takes the guess work out of improving the Value-added-Delivery System essential to the success of an organization.

Start with a small (1 or 2 VADS) project. This will allow the team to accomplish a project in a short time frame (5 to 6 weeks) and demonstrate quick results. It will also provide a framework for the team to identify shortfalls in its understanding and execution of HELIX. This will add to the team's confidence level, provide experiential learning and add value to the organization without a large investment.

Be sure to properly groom 1 to 3 HELIX facilitators. Competent facilitators are critical to the HELIX project's success.

Finally, stay close to the project's progress. Have weekly

conversations with the project team and the knowledge workers. Be sensitive to their feelings about the HELIX process and the actual results of what is being produced. In doing so, the team and the project participants will sense the caring, commitment and leadership needed to achieve effective change. The organization will benefit from the improved profits that accompany increased morale and increased efficiency.

Thank you again. I wish you great success.

Now is the time to take action.
Begin the quest to improve your
organization today.

Appendix

Influential Reading and Listening

The following are some of the books (printed and on tape) that have influenced my thinking and have helped me to add value to HELIX. They are listed here for the readers further study.

Title	Author	Publisher & ISBN
Are Your Lights On?	Donald C. GauseGerald M. Weinberg	Dorset House Publishing 0-932633-16-1
Breakthrough Thinking	Denis WaitleyRobert R. Tucker	Nightingale-Conant
Brining Out the Best in People	Alan Loy McGinnis	Nightingale-Conant
Coping With Difficult People	Robert M. Branson Ph.D.	Nightingale-Conant
Dinosaur Brains	Albert J. BernsteinSydney Craft Rozen	John Wiley & Sons
Emotional Intelligence	Daniel Goleman	Audio Renaissance Tapes 1-55927-382-8

Influential Reading (cont.)

Title	Author	Publisher & ISBN
Frontal Attack	Richard Buskirk	Nightingale-Conant
Getting to Yes	Robert Fischer William Ury	Nightingale-Conant
How to Be a Great Communicator	Nido Qubein	Nightingale-Conant
How to Handle Conflict & Manage Anger	Denis Waitley	Nightingale-Conant 0-671-89481-1
How to Work a Room	Susan Roane	Warner Books 0-446-39065-8
Jesus, CEO	Laurie Beth Jones	Simon & Schuster Audio 0-671-52032-6
Leadership When the Heat's On	Danny Cox	The Audio Partners 0-945353-95-2
Leading	Philip B. Crosby	McGraw-Hill 0-07-014567-9
Learning to Lead	Jay A. Conger	Josey Bass 1-55542-474-0
Lessons in Success and Leadership	Philip Caldwell	Nightingale-Conant
Management of the Absurd	Richard Farson	Simon & Schuster Audio 0-671-56907-4

Influential Reading (cont.)

Title	Author	Publisher & ISBN
Positioning	Nido Qubein	Nightingale-Conant
Relationship Strategies	Tony Alessandra Ph.D.	Alessandra & Associates
Running Things	Philip B. Crosby	McGraw Hill 0-07-014513-X
Skills for Success	Adele Scheele, Ph.D.	Nightingale-Conant
The Holly Bible	King James Version	Thomas Nelson & Sons
The Power of Focused Thinking	Edward de Bono	International Center for Creative Thinking 0-9615400-6-0
The Science of Self Discipline	Kerry L. Johnson	Nightingale-Conant
The Screwtape Letters	C.S. Lewis	Audio Lecture 0-944993-15-X
The Secrets of Power Persuasion	Roger Dawson	Nightingale-Conant
The Subliminal Winner	Denis Waitley Thomas Budzynski, Ph.D.	Nightingale-Conant
The Tao of Physics	Fritjof Capra	Audio Renaissance Tapes
A Fifth Discipline	Peter Senge	Doubleday 0-385-26095-4
The -Working Leader	Leonard R. Sayles	The Free Press 0-02-927755-8
Winning Through Teamwork	Lawrence M. Miller	Nightingale-Conant

It all boils down to this: The more you give The more you get. The more you get The more you have to give

GLOSSARY OF TERMS

Below are key terms used throughout the book. The definitions are provided in context to their usage within the book are not to be confused with technical dictionary descriptions.

A

Alignment; The state where an organization's intent, ability and outcomes consistently meet the expectations of its stakeholders.

B

Beginning Status; The status of a Value-added Delivery System before it starts a normal cycle. The point in time prior to a primary object having any status within a VADS cycle. Found on the WFL2 model.

C

Change Analysis; A model providing a contrast between a situation in terms of what is measurably wrong with it and its attributes if it were totally acceptable.

Collaboration; The process of two or more people working together, sharing ideas and techniques with the joint intent to achieve a shared vision or outcome.

Consensus; The result of two or more people agreeing on an idea, result or course of action.

D

Diagnostic Work Session; A group activity where the information collected at a facilitation work session is reviewed and tested by the HELIX project team

Discovery; The process of allowing people to pursue a direction without complete knowledge of what lies ahead, but with the hope and intent that the effort will yield impressive results for the sponsoring or targeted stakeholders.

Downsizing; A concept made popular and used in the 1990's for growing a competitive advantage through the elimination of employees from the workforce. The concept was subsequently abandoned when organizations realized that shrinking and growing were not simultaneously compatible.

E

Ending Status; The last status a VADS cycle can have. The last status the primary object of a VADS cycle can have. The point in which the primary object of a VADS cycle can no longer be changed or transformed. Found on the WFL2 model.

Equilibrium; A condition where the variables involved in a change to an organization are counter balanced.

Existing Situation; The first column of a change analysis. A statement that describes, in measurable terms, what is going wrong with a process in terms of why it is bad, when it happens, who it happens too, how much it costs, etc.

F

Facilitation; The act of drawing out affably, courteously and graciously without thoughtlessness

Facilitation Work Session; A group activity where information is collected from a group of cross functional knowledge workers by a facilitator and placed into various HELIX models.

Failure Analysis; A diagnostic technique used on a Proposed WFL2 to identify, quantify and resolve potential failures in object transformations.

Focus Group; A team of knowledge workers who have a shared experience on how a specific VADS works and work together in facilitation work sessions to discover ways to improve a VADS in a way that is consistent with the business objectives of the organization.

Focused Urgency; the process of acting with deliberate dispatch on goals that are important.

H

HELIX; A complete and practical method for aligning strategic direction with the Value-added Delivery Systems used to provide value to stakeholders.

Homeostasis; An organisms natural response toward resisting change and maintaining its current state of equilibrium.

K

Knowledge Summary; A form completed by a HELIX project team where relevant observations from facilitation work sessions recorded,

Knowledge Worker; A person who has direct experience in the performance of a set of tasks and procedures contained within a VADS.

L

Lapsed Time; The number of minutes, hours or days that pass during the performance of a phase within a VADS cycle. Found on the WFL2 model.

Level 1 Workflow Model; A model used to depict the communications and objects shared between process groups in order to complete a cycle of a VADS.

Level 2 Workflow Model; A model used to depict the phases, procedures and object transformations required to successfully complete a VADS cycle.

Level of Effort; The amount of time expended by a person(s) in order to complete a phase of a VADS cycle. Found on the WFL2 model.

O

Object; A subject or grouping of information that is critical to the processing and sharing of information throughout a VADS cycle. Typically objects take the form of a document or transmission of data.

Object Transformation; The change that occurs to the status of an object as it moves from one VADS phase to the next.

P

Preliminary Goal; The knowledge worker's consensus as to what a situation might look like if it in a more perfect environment. Provides measurements as to cost, benefit, time, etc.

Primary Object; The focal point of a VADS. The critical subject matters or information that must be successfully transformed during a VADS cycle in order for the VADS to successfully complete.

Procedure; A step found on the WFL2 model depicting a specific action to be taken in order to transform a primary or secondary object within a VADS cycle.

R

Return on Investment (ROI); The amount of money or other value received over and above the original amount invested. Usually expressed as a percentage of the original investment received on an annual basis.

S

Stakeholders: People and organizations that receive or hope to receive value from an organization. Typically comprised of owners, customers, employees, community and mission critical vendors.

Strategic direction; the path an organization chooses to follow in order to achieve its vision of a future organizational state that is superior to the current state.

V

Value-added Delivery Systems: VADS; The cross functional - end to end - business processes within an organization that are performed on a recurring basis with the intent of providing one or more stakeholders with a specific, predefined outcome.

W

WFL1; See Level 1 Workflow Model

WFL2; See Level 2 Workflow Model

Work Session; Facilitation Work Session; A group activity where information is collected from a group of cross functional knowledge workers by a facilitator and placed into various HELIX models.

Work Session; Diagnostic Work Session; A group activity where the information collected at a facilitation work session is reviewed and tested by the HELIX project team.

INDEX

A

Add value --1;19;21;34;40;58;65;82;103;105;162*See also* See VADS
Alignment --viii;x;1;13;17;26;31;58;63;74;76;78;82;103;104;109;
    142;150;151;157

B

Beginning Status --129
Business objectives --69;74;150

C

CA --117;143;146;149
Change Analysis --49;51;52;53;61;73;93;108;109;116;117;118;119;
    120;128;132;134;142;145;146;149
Collaboration --24;27;31;58;80;161
Consensus --1;5;26;33;40;41;50;108;110;119;152;157;160

D

Diagnostic Work Session --109;110;141;144;152
Diagnostic Work Sessions --110
discover --22;25;26;28;58;60;78;101;133;161
Discover / Discovery --4;5
Downsizing --12;22;98

E

Ending Status --129
Equilibrium --44;45;46
Existing Situation --49;50;117;134

F

Facilitation --13;108;115;152*See also* See Listening
Facilitation Work Session --109;115;121;128;137;138;140;142;145;151
Factor # 1 — The Principle of Making a Differen --19
Factor # 2 — The Principle of Value-added D --21
Factor # 3 — The Principle of Discovery --25
Factor # 4 — The Principle of Collaboration --27
Factor # 5 — The Principle of Context --31
Factor # 6 — The Principle of Conditioning for --43

The HELIX Factor

H

K

L

O

P

FOR MORE INFORMATION ON HELIX,

CONTACT

The Natural Intelligence Press

P.O. Box 785

Marmora, 08223 NJ

Or Call

Phone: (609) 861-3085

For Orders and Inquiries

FAX: (800) 243-9024
Email: mike_wood@msn.com